Should Christians be Torah Observant?

The Workbook!

Carmen Welker

Printed in the United States of America

ISBN 978-1-62374-009-2

Unless otherwise noted:

Tanakh ("Old Testament") scriptures and any accompanying footnotes are by Andrew Gabriel Roth, used with permission. *B'rit Chadashah* ("New Testament") scripture quotations are from the Aramaic English New Testament (AENT), copyright 2008, is with permission. All rights reserved.

2nd edition, March 2013

Sapphire
SapphirePubs.com

Dedication

This book is dedicated to my:

- ❖ My very loving and supportive husband, Bill, without whom this project would not have been possible. And to:

- ❖ Ellis Ipock who led me to the "right place at the right time" in January 1995 and was instrumental in "jump-starting" my glorious journey with God.

- ❖ Andrew Gabriel Roth who allowed me unlimited permission to quote from his Aramaic English New Testament (AENT) and other writings.

About the front cover

I chose for my book cover the menorah because it not only represents one of the oldest symbols of the Jewish faith but it is the **only** symbol YAHWEH, our Creator, designed Himself (Exodus 25:31-40). The menorah is also said to be a symbol of Israel's mission to be "a light unto the nations" (Isaiah 42:6).

Please note the menorah on the front cover, made of pure 24k gold, was painstakingly made to look like the original in the First Temple. It is currently on display in The Cardo in Jerusalem in a protected Plexiglas room. Constructed by The Temple Institute of the Old City, it is the actual menorah that will be used when the Third Temple is built. For more information, please visit the Third Temple website:

http://www.thirdtemple.com/OldCity/gallery.htm

Table of Contents

Foreword

This eye-opening study, depending on how much time and work you do during each session, can take as little as one week to complete, or it may take up to eight weeks, if done at the rate of one chapter per week. Please pray and ask the Holy Spirit for guidance before the beginning of each session, and don't hesitate to verify in the Scriptures everything you read and learn in "Should Christians be Torah Observant? – The Workbook!".... because, if something cannot be verified in the Bible, it isn't of God!

Each chapter ends with a series of pertinent questions designed to help you assess what you know about God and the Bible. When you are finished, you may compare your answers to those provided in Appendix of this workbook.

May the God of Abraham, Isaac and Jacob be with you as you embark on this exciting journey into Truth!

> *"Wisdom is calling! Understanding is raising her voice!"* (*Proverbs 8:1*, CJB)

> *"All the words from my mouth are righteous; nothing false or crooked is in them. They are all clear to those who understand and straightforward to those who gain knowledge."* (*Proverbs 8:8-9*, CJB)

This study is for those who are serious *about wanting a closer relationship to God...For those who recognize that "something" is missing in the church and desire a deeper relationship with God...For those who are ready, willing and able to move on to spiritual maturity by opening their minds to some powerful truths!*

Most Christians and Catholics wish to have a closer relationship with God; but, unfortunately, many don't realize they have been adhering to the doctrines of man, including the much-misunderstood writings of the Apostle Paul – ideas and theologies that sound good but in actuality, miss the mark.

That is what this study is designed to reveal and correct.

Here is a quick overview of what you are about to learn. Some of this will sound very strange, but it will all become crystal clear in the end!

- Beginning in the Garden of Eden, YAHWEH handed down guidelines for moral, holy living (His do's and don'ts). These guidelines are called "Torah" or "Instructions in Righteousness" that can be found in the first five Books of the Bible (Genesis through Deuteronomy). Once Adam and Eve were kicked out of the Garden for disobedience, YAHWEH's Torah commands began to increase. Included in these commands was the requirement to sacrifice innocent animals to atone for sins.

- As the earth's population increased, so did the Torah commands. At first, it was up to each individual to act as his own "priest" and perform his own animal sacrifices, but as the population grew, YAHWEH established a priesthood via the Tribe of Levi to intervene on the community's behalf.

- Many Torah commands were only for the priests; some were only for men, while others were only for women. Many commands have "forever" or "throughout your generations" attached to them, and those are still valid today for ALL who believe in the God of Abraham!

- Many believe Torah is only for the Jews, but the fact is, there were no Jews until Jacob begat his son Yehudah (Judah) from where the term "Jew" originated – yet **everyone** who believed in YAHWEH up until then was Torah observant….

- Two thousand years ago, YAHWEH sent His "Son" in human form to basically "put a Face on God" – someone who could show mankind who God was, personally demonstrate how to worship and obey Him, and ultimately to martyr Himself as our Final **Sin** Sacrifice. YAHWEH never demanded human sacrifices, but His Son CHOSE to die on our behalf, voluntarily taking the sin of the world upon His own shoulders (Isaiah 53: 5-12.) He did not come to replace His Father YAHWEH or abolish Torah!

- The Messiah who briefly walked this earth two thousand years ago was not called "Jesus" but "Yeshua" – which in Hebrew means "YAHWEH is Salvation." Yeshua – a Human with a divine Nature (an "arm" of YAHWEH, Isaiah 53:1) – was a Torah observant, *tallit*-wearing, Seventh Day Sabbath and Biblical Feast-keeping, kosher Jew who came to do His Father's will, proclaim the Kingdom of YAHWEH and to show mankind how to properly obey His will…and then to die on the behalf of a lost humanity that had totally strayed from Him over the millennia. He even said why He came: *"And Y'shua said to them that, 'It is necessary for me to preach to other cities the Kingdom of Elohim, for because this reason I have been sent.'"* (Luke 4:43)

- Many Christians – especially some "white supremacist" types – are angry with "the Jews" because "the Jews killed Jesus." Although it was "the Jews" who got the ball rolling concerning Yeshua's murder, it cannot be overlooked that it was the Gentile Romans who arrested Him, stripped Him, spat upon Him, flogged Him, ripped out His beard, put a crown of thorns upon His head, mocked Him, and ultimately nailed Him to the cross! Furthermore, there was a "mixed crowd" cheering on His execution (see Matthew 27), not just "the Jews."

- If Yeshua had not chosen to do His Father's will by dying on that fateful day, the world would have **no** Sin Sacrifice!

- It was because of "the Jews" that knowledge of YAHWEH and Yeshua came into the world when they were scattered into the nations. Had it not been for them, knowledge of YAHWEH would have remained imprisoned in tiny, little Israel and the world would still be writhing in paganism today. Instead of wasting energy hating "the Jews" the world should be thanking them for introducing them to the God of Abraham, Isaac and Jacob.

Please understand, the purpose of this study is not to attack Christians but, to reveal that Christianity, in general, has twisted the Word of God. My desire is to put Christians back on the right track by asking you to read and attempt to understand Bible scriptures in context….

And so, without further ado, let's begin! May the Holy Spirit guide you on this wonderful journey into the Torah!

Prologue

"Something" missing in the Church....

I was 44 years old before I finally found my way to God. It happened when the Holy Spirit grabbed hold of me one cold winter day in 1995, in a small country Baptist church in Missouri where the Pastor, Wil Pounds, just "happened" to say all the right things to make me realize I would be more than just worm fodder when I died.

The comments that actually pushed me "over the edge" went something like this: "Let's suppose for a moment you died today and stood before the Lord God and He asked you, 'Why should I let you into My heaven?' What would you say to Him? Would your response be something like, 'I am a religious person trying to live a Christian life the best I can'? Or, 'I go to church, give to the poor, help people in need, and have always tried to be a good person'?"

My eyes were wide as saucers as I contemplated Wil's question, and I quickly decided, "Yes, that's pretty much what my answer would be. What else could you say? What else is there?" But Wil's next comment knocked me for the proverbial loop: "If your answer to any of these questions was 'yes' then you'd be wrong because NONE of those things would get you into heaven! The **only** thing that gets you into heaven is your belief in the shed blood at the cross – by faith in Jesus Christ who died on the cross paying the penalty for our sins...."

I was stunned! Until that day, I had never understood why anyone in their right mind would be willing to die a hideous death for the world at large, or how that particular death was supposed to affect my relationship with God. But when Wil's words hit home something inside me "clicked" and I realized for the first time in my life that Jesus was our FINAL SIN SACRIFICE; He was the divine Being who forever abolished the need for animal sin sacrifices God had always required of His people since the day Adam and Eve were evicted from the Garden!

As someone who was born Jewish in a tiny town in post-war Germany where God was basically dead, I knew next to nothing about the Bible and never really cared to; and so naturally I was taken aback over the things Wil was espousing. I had always "believed" in God and figured that, while He knew I was sinning, He forgave me because He also understood I was a mere human who had already been through hell on Earth, and so He surely wouldn't condemn me there for eternity.

Yet, there I was in all my middle-aged glory, finally discovering that I had a Savior whose atoning death had relieved me of my need to hide from God anymore, or agonize over the willful things I had done to displease Him. Until then, I had been floundering around in my daily routine, trying to recover from a lifetime of endless trials and tribulations, and attempting to fill that "little hole in my soul" with worldly stuff….

In the following weeks after I "got saved" Pastor Wil began tutoring his new "baby Christian" relentlessly – and, of course, I was a virtual sponge, learning everything I possibly could from this amazing teacher. I faithfully completed all the workbooks he recommended and also attended Sunday school and evening Bible studies wherever I could find them. Over the course of about a year, I generally drove Wil crazy with non-stop questions, while he introduced me to a brand new world designed to show me what being "born again" was all about. I simply couldn't get enough of Jesus!

It wasn't long before I became Bible literate enough to begin asking some really tough questions. For instance, I quickly came to realize that the entire Bible was all about the Jews and Israel, and I became confused – not to mention worried – about the idea that my brethren would all go to hell because they didn't believe that Jesus was "God Incarnate." I remember wondering if the Jews (who already believed in the God of Abraham, Isaac and Jacob) were God's "Chosen People" then why would they end up in hell just because they didn't "believe in Jesus?" Did everybody BEFORE Jesus go to hell because they didn't have a chance to believe in Him? I mean, neither Enoch (Genesis 5:24) nor Elijah (2 Kings 2:11) "believed in Jesus" and yet they both went to heaven….

Eventually, I also began to wonder why the church felt that Jesus had "done away with the law" because, according to what I was gleaning from the Bible, "the law" was Torah, God's original **divine** teaching and instruction, outlined in the first five Books of the Bible. The Books of Leviticus, Numbers and Deuteronomy go into agonizing detail on who God is and how to worship Him, and how we are to celebrate the Feasts (all of which foreshadow Jesus). They outline how He wants us to behave, how we are to treat each other, and even what we can and cannot eat. Without the Torah, we wouldn't have any of these guidelines which comprise our ONLY perfect blueprint for safe, moral and godly living – so why would God's original teachings and commands become null and void just because Jesus' human body died? Why would we want them to become null and void?

Throughout my "Baby Christian" days the Holy Spirit kept telling me that Jesus was our SIN Sacrifice, not someone who came to replace God the Father and His original teachings. After all, in Old Testament times, the animals that were killed to atone for man's sins covered our SINS only; their deaths didn't magically abolish any of God's commandments, so why would the death of His Son? **Covenants** changed, but God's Torah did not. The "New Testament" constantly refers to the "Old Testament" which contains all the original teachings and the "Thus saith the Lord" verses, not the other way around. It simply does not make any sense to insist that just because Jesus died, all of God's original instructions to mankind supposedly went out the window. It makes no sense to think the seventh day Sabbath which our Creator instituted and personally observed (Genesis 2:2) was changed to the first day, or that pork and shellfish somehow became "clean" just because Jesus died!

In Matthew 5:17 Jesus even said: *"Do **not** think that I have come to loosen Torah or the prophets, I have **not** come to loosen but to fulfill."* To me that indicated a beginning, not an ending or a "loosening" ("abolishing"). If Jesus didn't "loosen" then "fulfill" could NOT mean "put an end to."

Something else that bothered me was the fact that the Church considers God's original teachings a "curse." How could anything God ever taught be a curse? If Torah is a curse, then why do both Isaiah and Micah tell us that "in the last days" Torah/the Law **will** be taught upon Jesus' return: *The law will go out from Zion, the word of the LORD from Jerusalem.* (NASB) Will we be living "under a curse" in the future when Jesus returns to rule and reign? If so, why is everyone so eager for "the Rapture?"

I also noticed that the Torah contains several "forever" commands, such as the Biblical Feasts which the Bible clearly states are to be observed FOREVER. But, whenever I asked a pastor or Bible study teacher about this, they always insisted that, as a Christian, I wouldn't have to worry about them because the "Old Testament" commands were directed only at the Jews. How could this be, I wondered, since we all worship the **same God** who had specifically instructed the "foreigners" and all who "attached themselves" to Israel to do **exactly** as the Jews (Numbers 15:13-16)? Shouldn't those tenets apply equally to everyone, or did God at some point hand down two different sets of rules?

Millions of questions raced through my mind and soon I began to feel that "something wasn't right" in the Church. Despite the fact that I was now "saved" I felt unfulfilled somehow, yet could not figure out why. Wherever I turned with my myriad questions, I ended up being hammered with the mantras, "The law is a curse" and "Jesus nailed it to the cross"….or , "Well, PAUL said…."

For months, I studied everything I could get my hands on, eagerly soaking up the Bible, asking questions and mulling over certain Church teachings that didn't seem to make sense. For some reason I couldn't shake the nagging feeling that, although I had always "believed" in God on some level – this "Jesus" just didn't seem like the same God who had given Man His original teaching and instruction. Nothing against any of the pastors I have ever studied under and learned from, but what I thought I was reading in the Bible didn't exactly match what I was hearing from the podium….

For instance, the Gospels are clear that Jesus kept the seventh day Sabbath and the Biblical feasts as His Father commanded. I saw no place in the Bible that suggested those things had been done away with, even in the writings of Paul. As a matter of fact, unlike most people who seem to believe that Paul was against "the law," I personally felt that his writings had been misunderstood because I, even as a "baby Christian" could see clearly that Paul, like Jesus, was a Torah observant Jew who upheld the Law. He actually said so in Romans 3:31: *Do we then nullify the Law through faith? May it never be! On the contrary, we establish the Law.* (NASB) If we **establish** the Law, then we can't at the same time insist it's been abolished. Furthermore, 1 John 3 clearly says that **sin** is "lawlessness" – which means "the Law" could not have been abolished at the cross!

1 John 3:4 Everyone who sins breaks the law; in fact, sin is lawlessness. 5 But you know that he appeared so that he might take away our sins. And in him is no sin. 6 No one who lives in him keeps on sinning. No one who continues to sin has either seen him or known him. (NIV)

And so I remained frustrated until God caused me to move to Colorado in 1996, where I eventually got the answers to all my questions after discovering "Messianic Judaism" – a belief based on the idea that the Bible is one, continuous, "God-breathed" entity as opposed to two, separate "testaments" wherein one supersedes the other.

Through some miraculous circumstances, I ended up in a Torah class learning things I could have never gleaned from a regular church setting. For instance, I learned that Jesus had come to preach and Good News and proclaim the Kingdom of God, not to "abolish" anything (Luke 4:43, Acts 28:23)! I learned that much of God's divine instruction in righteousness has been mistranslated because of the intricacies of the Hebrew language, and that Paul's teachings have been very much misunderstood because they are being viewed through a "Greek/Gentile" mindset.

I learned that the Father's Name is יהוה (the Hebrew letters, read right-to-left, Yud-Hey-Vav-Hey = YHWH, pronounced YAH-WEH), and His Son's given Hebrew Name was actually ישוע which transliterated into English is Y'shua or Yeshua, and means "YAHWEH is Salvation." (Yeshua isn't that hard to pronounce in ANY language, and I wondered why "the world" had seen fit to change it.) Not only had His Name been changed, but also the dates of His birth, death and resurrection which are clearly outlined in the Bible! I also learned the difference between the "Hebrew" and the "Greek" mindsets which helped to clarify why "Jesus" in no way resembles the Torah observant, seventh day Sabbath and Feast keeping, kosher Jew who walked this Earth two thousand years ago….

And now, I want to pass this knowledge on to you. If, after you read the following pages you still don't believe that Christians should be Torah observant, at least you will be able to make up your mind from a more informed perspective. May God bless and enlighten you as you read and answer the questions posed in this workbook.

Ready? Let's begin!

Chapter 1

Torah is not "legalism" or a "curse" – Torah consists of God's Instructions in Righteousness!

*Matthew 7:21. It will not be that just anyone who says to me "My master, my master!" will enter the Kingdom of Heaven, **but whoever does the will of my Father who is in heaven.** 22. Many will say to me in that day, "My master, my master! By your name, have we not prophesied? And by you name have we cast out demons? And by your name have we done many miracles?" 23. And then I will profess to them that from everlasting, I have not known you. Depart from me, you workers of iniquity!*

Every believer owes it to him or herself to ask the question: "Am I really worshipping God according to what the Bible says, or am I blindly following Man? I mean, how do I know for sure that my particular denomination is the one God approves of, and whether or not we are 'doing it right'? "

The answer, of course, is: MAN came up with all the denominations and NONE of them are "doing it right!" Man with his limited human mindset has put God in a box and attempted to force Him to fit into the "theology du jour." Rather than to consult the Holy Spirit to help him understand God and the Bible, Man has picked his way through the Scriptures in search of whatever supports his particular premise. The result has been myriad "denominations" (there are more than 1,500 Christian faith groups in North America alone) each claiming to be "the right" one....

It's no wonder then that, in recent years, many Christians have gone "church shopping" and/or completely exited the church altogether because they felt "something was missing." Some ultimately found themselves in "Messianic" congregations where a "whole new world" opened up when they discovered that what they had been missing was a working knowledge of Torah, the first five Books which contain God's original, divine instructions without which Man would have **no** blueprint for moral behavior.

If you are among those Christians who have felt a certain "nudging" in your spiritual life, this book will serve as a true eye-opening experience, because you'll find that "Torah" is not what you thought! Torah is not "legalism" as the Church insists; it is the Word of God. Legalism consists of the **man-made** concepts which crept into Torah....Yet, many Christians are quick to point out that those who believe in being Torah observant are "under the law" or practicing "legalism." Nothing could be further from the truth!

*James 4:11. Speak not against each other, my Brothers; for he that speaks against his brother, or judges his brother speaks against Torah and judges Torah. **And if you judge Torah, you are not a doer of Torah, but its judge.** 12. There is one Torah-giver and Judge who can make alive and (can) destroy: but who are you that you judge your neighbor?*

Before we go any further, I'd like to make it perfectly clear that this book is **not** intended to "bash" our Christian or Catholic brethren, nor does it advocate that Torah "saves" us; **only** the shed blood of Messiah has that power! You have the choice to study the contents of this book to learn what Torah is, and then make up your own mind as to whether to accept or reject it! I am also not suggesting that "Messianic" teachers have cornered the market on Truth *because Satan has infiltrated the "Messianic Movement" just as much as any other "religion."* There are plenty of "Messianic" teachers and "rabbis" in the world whose teachings are completely off the mark because, rather than to teach TRUTH, they have inserted their own carnal opinions into the Word! What I am attempting to get across is that believers in Messiah must begin to read the Bible for what it actually says, and adhere to YAHWEH's teachings instead of blindly swallowing whatever their respective priests or pastors espouse.

This study will demonstrate that Christians have misunderstood God's concept of "the Law" and, as a result, they are missing out on many blessings – not to mention, the "bigger picture" in the grand scheme of things – which includes the misleading "Jesus nailed it to the cross" idea that has caused many to confuse legalism (the traditions and opinions of men) with the actual commands of YAHWEH.

YAHWEH is the name God revealed both to Abram in Genesis 13 and later to Moses in Exodus 3. It is a transliteration of the Hebrew letters comprising our Creator's Name: יהוה = **Yud-Hey-Vav-Hey** = YHWH, pronounced YAH-WEH. These letters were inspired by the *Ruach haKodesh* (Holy Spirit) to appear nearly 7,000 times in the *Tanakh* ("Old Testament"), yet the Name is nowhere to be found in our English versions except where it appears in an abbreviated form at the end of the word "Halleluyah." English translators were guilty of adding to our Creator's Word by replacing His personal Name with the capital letters LORD, GOD and the hybrid "Jehovah". (Ironically, traditional Jews know His Name but they refuse to utter it for fear of mispronouncing or misspelling it....)

Genesis 13:1. And Abram went up out of Egypt, he, and his wife, and all that he had, and Lot with him, into the South. 2. And Abram was very rich in cattle, in silver, and in gold. 3. And he went on his journeys from the South even to Beth-el, to the place where his tent had been at the beginning, between Beth-el and Ai, 4. to the place of the altar, which he had made there at the first. **And there Abram called on the name of YHWH.**

Exodus 3:13. Moshe said to Elohim, "Look, when I appear before the people of Isra'el and say to them, 'The Elohim of your ancestors has sent me to you'; and they ask me, 'What is his name?' what am I to tell them?" 14. Elohim said to Moshe, "Ehyeh Asher Ehyeh [I am Who I am, I will be What I am]," and added, "Here is what to say to the people of Isra'el: 'Ehyeh [I Am or I Will Be] has sent me to you.'" **15. Elohim said then to Moshe, "Say this to the people of Isra'el: YAHWEH [He is], the Elohim of your fathers, the Elohim of Avraham, the Elohim of Yitz'chak and the Elohim of Ya'akov, has sent me to you.' This is my name for all time; this is how generation after generation is to remember Me."**

NOTE: *Ehyeh Asher Ehyeh* is "to be" in the first person, where YAHWEH says in essence, "this is the Name I call Myself." It is the fact that YAHWEH says "My Name for myself is simply that I exist" which is the extra revelation given to Moshe. However, Abram was also told in Genesis 13:1-4 that Elohim was called "יהוה". In that case, YAHWEH is really "He is", or the male third person form of *Ehyeh*. So Abram only knew "He is/was/will be" {YHWH} as the Name, but Moshe understood the meaning behind the Name, that YAHWEH applies it to Himself directly. As a result, there is no contradiction between YAHWEH revealing Himself as YAHWEH to Abram and making the meaning of His Name fully known to Moshe.

The bottom line is, we are living in the end times as outlined in the Books of Daniel and Revelation, and it is imperative that church leaders begin to re-examine their stance on whether or not they are teaching according to YAHWEH's instructions. By ignoring "the bigger picture" pastors all over the world are guilty of leading people astray – and their flocks are guilty of **allowing** themselves to be led astray!

This is not to imply that Christians (and Catholics and everyone else who believes in Jesus) don't "love the Lord." However, by ignoring Torah they are guilty of willfully disobeying some of YAHWEH's "forever" commands, which puts them in danger of being considered "lukewarm" on Judgment Day (Revelation 3:16), and consequently ending up the "least" in the Kingdom (Matthew 5:19).

Therefore, this study makes two bold suggestions (which will probably make more sense to you once you've completed it):

(1) Pastors: Those pastors who desire to be accurate, on-the-mark stewards of YAHWEH's Word need to prayerfully reconsider what they were taught in seminary or other Christian settings, and re-examine the Bible with "new eyes" to see whether or not their teachings and actions line up with the Word of God – beginning with the rules, regulations, works and theologies of their own respective denominations (all of which were man-made).

(2) Congregations: If pastors refuse to follow the example of Yeshua (our Savior's given, Hebrew Name which means "YAHWEH Saves" or "YAHWEH is Salvation"), our Torah observant, seventh day Sabbath and Feast keeping Savior, then their congregations have the responsibility to exit the churches, forget about what they've been taught and, with the help of the Holy Spirit, begin their own journeys into The Word! Matthew 7:13 tells us that most people will NOT be entering through the "narrow gate that leads to life" and so it is imperative that you at least be able to make up your own mind about Torah from an **informed** perspective, before you decide to accept or reject it.

YAHWEH said: *My people are destroyed for a lack of knowledge....* (Hosea 4:6). To become the well-versed witness He wants you to be, you first need to figure out precisely what "knowledge" you have missed out on – starting with the fact that Christians who have been taught "Jesus nailed it to the cross" don't seem to understand exactly **what** was nailed to the cross. They are under the erroneous impression that this refers to God's original divine instructions, even though there is nothing in Scripture to substantiate this idea!

Having said that, let's discuss exactly what was "nailed to the cross"....

Yeshua "nailed to the cross" *the requirement to provide sacrifices to atone for our sins.* That is all. He did not come to replace YAHWEH the Father, nor did He ever suggest that He came to do away with His Father's rules and regulations nor any of the original teachings; on the contrary, He came to impress upon us the need to learn and obey the very Torah that He Himself observed and enforced!

Isaiah 9:6. For a child is born to us, a son is given to us; the government will rest on his shoulders, and he will be given the name Pele-Yo'etz El Gibbor Avi-'Ad Sar-Shalom [Awe-Inspiring Counselor, Mighty El, Father of Eternity, Prince of Peace], 7. of the increase of his rule there shall be no end and he will rule on David's throne and over David's domain, to establish it and propagate it through justice and righteousness from now on and forever. The zeal of YAHWEH-Tzva'ot [YAHWEH OF HOSTS] will bring this about.

NOTE: (Isaiah 9:6-7 is shown as verses 5-6 in some Bible versions.) The word *peleyoet* is used most often in a good sense to describe the power and majesty of YAHWEH (Exodus 15:11) and in a bad sense to display the depth of our sin in YAHWEH's eyes (Lamentations 1:9). Either way, it seems that "wonderful" as the meaning of *peleyoet* in Isaiah 9:6, and its homophonic variations, does not carry the total depth of the Hebrew meaning. The counsel described here is of a supernatural nature beyond that of the best human insights. As a result, Andrew Gabriel Roth found "awe-inspiring" more accurate since this tells the reader to look for the "wonder" outside of their own experience and be "inspired" in the manner of YAHWEH intervening in history for our benefit.

Yeshua worked very hard to make us aware of the man-made concepts and ideologies that had crept into YAHWEH's Word, and to show us how to discern and weed out the endless barrage of rabbinical laws that kept in bondage the ancient believers. Ironically, today's Christian pastors are guilty of perpetuating their own "rabbinical" notions which include telling their congregations that "the law" was abolished, without even realizing they're talking about *GOD's* divine, eternal Laws!

As proof that "Jesus nailed it to the cross," however, pastors readily refer to the much mistranslated and misunderstood teachings of Paul which supposedly show that YAHWEH changed the seventh-day Sabbath to Sunday (the "first day"), render null and void the Biblical Feasts, and suggest Man can now eat pork and shellfish – and all this just because Yeshua died on the cross....

Why has hardly anyone questioned these supposed discrepancies or checked to see what the Bible actually says? How many have even noticed that Yeshua said He did **not** come to abolish Torah?

Matthew 5:17. Do not think that I have come to loosen Torah or the prophets; I have not come to loosen but to fulfill. 18. For truly I say to you that until heaven and earth pass away not one Yodh or one stroke will pass from Torah until everything happens. 19. All who loosen, therefore, from one (of) these small commandments and teach thus to the sons of man, will be called little in the Kingdom of Heaven, but all who do and teach this will be called great in the Kingdom of Heaven. 20. For I say to you that unless your righteousness exceeds more than that of the scribes and the Pharisees, you will not enter the Kingdom of Heaven.

Has everything happened that must happen? Have heaven and earth passed away? If not, then why is the Church ignoring Torah? How do the concepts of "complete" or "fulfill" equate to "abolished or done away with"?

And how in the world did intelligent people ever allow themselves to be talked into the arrogant, impudent and rebellious idea that God's Law could **ever** be "a curse"? Or the belief that YAHWEH doesn't expect anything more of us than to "believe in Christ" while we're ignoring His commanded "forever" Feasts and instead, celebrating **man-made** "holy days" and traditions completely steeped in paganism?

Here's the sobering million dollar question: If you're among those who believe "the law is a curse," would you be willing to stake your eternal life on this philosophy without even bothering to take a second look at the Bible, just to make sure?

An example to illustrate Torah:

Good parents teach their children to obey some fundamental rules during their formative years. We teach them that touching a hot stove will burn their fingers, that trying to play with stray dogs might result in being bitten, or that it's dangerous to cross the street without first checking to see if a car is coming. We teach them necessary manners and show them how to get along with others, and to say "please" and "thank you"– basic rules of etiquette. The purpose of our careful tutelage is to raise decent human beings and to provide our offspring with knowledge they can carry with them forever; knowledge they can build on and eventually impart to their own kids. In other words, we give them a kind of "Torah"– a blueprint for moral and safe behavior.

Now, imagine, for instance, some flashy, charismatic person coming along and telling your children that whenever they reach the age of, say, 12, they will no longer be required to obey their parents and can do whatever they want, regardless of the consequences, because somehow the age of 12 magically negates everything their parents ever taught them. At age 12, according to this charismatic person, our children are "grown up" and no longer subject to their parents' rules and regulations. They can lie, steal, cheat, do drugs, have sex whenever and with whomever they want and cross the road without looking, and generally do whatever they desire because, after all, "you only live once." As humans who are born into sin (Genesis 3; Romans 3), our kids will naturally be drawn to this new liberty they think they've discovered, and so they begin to rebel because our rules and regulations are outdated and get in the way of their desires....

The problem is: Will our children's "new liberty" appeal to us parents? Of course not, because we know their actions will ultimately result in certain pain and/or death!

But isn't this exactly what we have done with the Word of YAHWEH by insisting "we are under grace" because "Jesus nailed it to the cross" and we're therefore not subject to God's Laws today? When and how did grace replace the need to obey the rules?

A favorite mantra of Christians is, "The law is written on our hearts!" Unfortunately, this is an untrue statement because, unless one has first **learned** YAHWEH's Laws, one cannot have them "written on their hearts".... It's like learning the alphabet; you have to have learned and memorized it before it's ever "written on your heart."

Thanks to the willful disobedience of Adam and Eve in the Garden of Eden, mankind is automatically born into sin (Romans 3:10 and 3:23); and so, contrary to popular opinion, human babies are **not** born with God's Torah engraved upon their hearts. Just as they must be taught that hot stoves are dangerous, they must first be taught to memorize

His do's and don'ts before ANYTHING is "written on their hearts" or committed to memory.

The Apostle Paul who, as I've suggested has been much misunderstood by the Christian population (which this study will demonstrate later on), said:

Romans 2:12. For those without Torah, who sin, will also perish without Torah; and those under the Torah, who sin, will be judged by the Torah. 13. For not the hearers of the Torah are righteous before Elohim; but the doers of the Torah are being made righteous. 14. For if Gentiles who have not the Torah shall, by their nature, do the things of the Torah; they, while without the Torah, become a Torah to themselves. 15. Additionally, they show the work of the Torah as it is inscribed on their hearts; and their conscience bears testimony to them, their own reflections rebuking or vindicating one another. 16. (And that vindication is for) in the day in which Elohim will judge the secret [actions] of men, as my tidings [teaches], by Y'shua the Mashiyach.

Please ask the *Ruach haKodesh* (Holy Spirit) to help you understand Romans 2:12-16 above, which was translated directly from Aramaic into English. You'll notice it does not in any way infer that believers don't need the Torah, but rather that, without divine guidance, they will make up their own rules and regulations and attempt to decipher "right from wrong" and "rebuke and vindicate" each other from a human standpoint.

A footnote from Roth's Aramaic English New Testament (AENT) referring to this scripture, says: "Paul does not suggest that Gentiles should spontaneously master the Torah. The point is they should learn the written Torah without distraction from Pharisaic traditions which are not rooted in the plain understanding of Torah."

At the beginning of this chapter, I used Matthew 7:21-23, which discusses how YAHWEH will reject the "workers of lawlessness." We need to honestly ask ourselves: Who are the "workers of lawlessness"? The answer is: Those who don't conform to God's Laws! It's hypocritical to think of ourselves as "saints" while we are guilty of willful and deliberate sinning through our refusal to conform to Elohim's Rules. According to the Merriam-Webster Dictionary sin is the "transgression of the law of God" (also see 1 John 3:4).

As Scripture affirms in several places, there is but **one** YAHWEH and **one** divine Instruction for the Jew and for the foreigner who has chosen to follow the God of Abraham, Isaac and Jacob. Isra'el was to be the example for all other nations to follow, not the sole user of the Torah.

Torah binds our relationship with God. It reveals who He is, explains how we are to worship Him, and shows how He wants us to live and behave according to His rules, which are designed with our welfare in mind. (And, as all good, God-fearing Christians should know, if we desire to have a relationship with God, we cannot pick and choose what we want to believe of the Bible! We must either accept **all** or none of it....)

The following pages will demonstrate how Christians, as a whole, are missing the "big picture" – and consequently, losing out on some of YAHWEH's blessings because they are ignoring Torah and adhering instead to the watered-down gospel started by the "Church fathers" who passed off as Truth their twisted understanding of the "Old Testament" and the teachings of our Savior, Yeshua haMashiyach (Jesus the Messiah).

Questions for Chapter 1

After reading the Prologue and Chapter 1 (and referring to your Bible), you should be able to answer the following questions. You may then compare your answers with those in the Appendix:

Question 1: Have you ever read the Bible from cover to cover? If not, how much of it have you actually read? Don't fudge; be brutally honest with yourself!

Question 2: According to the Scriptures, who is God and what is His Name?

Question 3: Who was the Son and why was He sent?

Question 4: Who was in charge of the universe while Yeshua was down here on earth?

Question 5: What was Jesus' given, Hebrew Name and what does it mean?

Question 6: Was Yeshua a Jew or Gentile? How do you know?

Question 7: Going by what you've learned so far, what is Torah? What is "legalism"? What do you think "being under the law" means?

Question 8: 1 John 3:4 tells us that sin is _____.

Question 9: Was the Son sent to abolish Torah? Why or why not?

Question 10: What, exactly, was "nailed to the cross?"

Question 11: In Matthew 5:17 Yeshua said He came not to "loosen but to fulfill" the Torah. What do you think He meant by that?

Question 12: Christians insist that "the law" is "written on our hearts" (Jeremiah 31:33-34; Romans 10:4-8) and therefore, the "OT" no longer pertains to them. How can man (who was born into sin) know what "the law" is, if he doesn't first study and learn to obey it?

Question 13: Why would God decide to destroy or change His mind about His own original divine instructions, without which we would have no guide to moral, holy living?

Question 14: Why are there so many and widely varying Christian denominations (not to mention, world "religions") each claiming to be "the right one"? What was Yeshua's particular "religion" or denomination?

Question 15: Why have so many Christian pastors over the years had to step down in shame from their self-indulgent pedestals for one reason or another? Weren't they doing God's will - and if not, why not? How come they were allowed to call themselves "men of the cloth" if they were off doing their own thing?

Question 16: Matthew 5:17-18 says: *Do not think that I have come to loosen Torah or the prophets; I have not come to loosen but to fulfill. For truly I say to you that until heaven and earth pass away not one Yodh or one stroke will pass from Torah until everything happens.* What does "loosen the Torah" mean to you? Has "everything" happened yet? Have heaven and earth passed away?

Chapter 2

Origin of the "Torah was nailed to the cross" idea

Notes:

There are plenty of "scholars" in this world who insist that Torah was only for the Jews and that anyone who belongs to Christ doesn't have to do anything but "believe." But what does the **Bible** say?

Read in context, we discover **there were no Jews** until after Jacob gave birth to his son, Judah who became the Tribe of Judah (Genesis 29:35; Matthew 1:1-2); yet **everyone**, beginning with Adam and Eve who had been given rules to follow (Genesis 2:16-17), and later Cain and Abel (Genesis 4) and Noah (Genesis 6), was Torah observant...which amply serves to negate the claim that Christians don't have to obey God's divine rules for righteousness! The term "Jews" has simply become a blanket description for all Israelites when, in actuality, only someone born into the Tribe of Judah can truly claim the title of "Jews." The *Tanach* (OT) shows that God's Chosen were called Hebrews (Genesis 14:13; also see the lives of Abraham, Isaac and Jacob in the *Tanach*).

Anyone who believes in the God of Abraham, Isaac and Jacob is to be Torah observant, and God even said so **four times in a row** in Numbers 15:13-16! YAHWEH chose Abraham because He wanted to (Deuteronomy 7:6-8) and He reiterated this in Jeremiah 31:32 by making His New

27

Covenant with the Houses of Israel and Judah - both of whom were Torah observant.

All First Century followers of Messiah Yeshua were Torah observant, and **you** should be, as well! Why? *Because believing Gentiles who are grafted into the Olive Tree (Israel) automatically become part of Israel!* Halleluyah! That doesn't mean they become "Hebrews" or "Jews" - but it does mean they are in royal company and complete God's Family! Please keep above facts in mind when reading the below which refers to "the Jews" in general terms.

To discover why Christians seem to believe they are exempt from Torah, all we need to do is to go back to the origin of the "Torah was nailed to the cross" myth – which was started by the "Church fathers"– men who basically claimed for their own the God of Abraham, Isaac and Jacob, and then, intentionally and/or unintentionally, stripped Him of His true, Biblical identity! This happened, in part, because they hated the Jews and anything Jewish, and because they, as Gentiles, viewed YAHWEH and the Bible through a Greek instead of a Hebrew mindset.

What is meant by "Hebrew mindset" vs. "Greek mindset"? It refers to the idea that there is a discrepancy between the Jewish and Christian concepts about life, God and Truth; in other words, they were "set" in their respective ways of thinking about these issues. In the mindset of the Hebrews, YAHWEH was the Creator. Period. Greeks, on the other hand, were Gentiles prone to be atheistic, agnostic, or into pagan gods – and that's why the Apostle Paul used different methods when he spoke to the Hebrew and Greek cultures.

Example: The "Greek" mindset visualizes a tattoo (or something similar) on the thigh of Jesus when he returns as "King of Kings, and Lord of Lords" (Revelation 19:11-13, 16), while the Hebrew mindset sees something deeper, more realistic, more Torah-based. The Hebrew mindset visualizes

Yeshua, the Torah observant Jewish Messiah wrapped in a tallit (prayer shawl) as He sits atop a white horse, headed back to Earth with the *tzitzits* (braids, knots, tassels) that fall across His thighs spelling out the Name of YAHWEH. (Each letter of the Hebrew alphabet has a numerical value and, consequently, the number of knots on the *tzitzits* on the four corners of a tallit, properly tied, spell out the name of YAHWEH. No tattoo required!)

Another example of a Hebrew as opposed to Greek mindset can be seen in the respective calendars/timelines. YAHWEH's timelines are amply evidenced throughout the Bible, whereas our Gregorian calendars are speckled with the names of pagan deities representing the days and months. According to YAHWEH, a "day" is **not** from midnight to midnight, but from "sunset to sunset" (Genesis 1:5). He called the days of the week the "first day," "second day," etc., whereas "the world" has named its days and months after pagan gods and goddesses.

Even though we're used to these names, we must search our hearts and be very honest with ourselves when posing the question: Since YAHWEH adamantly warned people about paganism and even put people to death for inserting anything unusual into our worship of Him (i.e., as in the case of Aaron's sons), why would He be happy about it today?

Anyway, the end result of these two different mindsets was devastating because, due to their misinterpretation, mistranslation, misunderstanding and misapplication of the Scriptures, Gentile church leaders managed to twist the Word of God and insert their own opinions into the equation. And their followers, of course, blindly accepted their "truth" as gospel. Down through the ages, rather than to examine the Bible and Messiah Yeshua's teachings for themselves, people continued to adhere to the teachings of the "Church fathers" without question, thus helping to perpetuate the "law is a curse" myth.

The following illustrations will give you a rough idea as to how the "Church fathers" influenced future generations of believers:

The devil made us do it!

Luke 4 tells us that Satan knocked himself out to tempt Yeshua. When that failed (despite the promise of all the kingdoms in the world), Satan basically went for human-kind's collective jugular, beginning with the insertion of false doctrine into the teachings of Yeshua; the main one being that "Christians" didn't need to be Torah observant.

The fact is, however, the Bible clearly shows that early Gentile believers **were** Torah observant – yet most Christians will adamantly refute this, using everything in their power to prove otherwise, and always presenting as their "indisputable proof" the misinterpreted teachings of Paul.

But please take a look at scriptures such as 1 Corinthians 5:8 where Paul, speaking of the Feast of Passover during which we are to rid ourselves of the leaven in our houses, says: "So let us celebrate the Seder"….(Some versions say, "keep the festival" or "celebrate the feast" which refers directly to Passover!) Paul said to celebrate Passover, not "Easter." Passover is one of the Feasts outlined in Torah (Exodus 12, Leviticus 23:4, Numbers 9).

Also, Acts 13:42-44 clearly shows that Gentiles in Antioch requested further instruction of Paul "on the next Sabbath" (YAHWEH's Sabbath is and always has been Saturday/the seventh day) and that almost the whole city arrived for the meeting on the next Sabbath. There were **never** any separate Sunday (first day) "Sabbath" meetings. In Yeshua's time on Earth both Jews and Gentiles regularly attended the synagogue for worship on the **seventh** day.

Some attempt to prove Paul held a "first day" Sabbath meeting in Acts 20:7, but the fact is, the group was participating in *Motzei Shabbat* which refers to the time in the evening immediately following Shabbat, when they gathered to break bread and continue to fellowship. In this particular passage we are told that Paul was leaving the next day, and so he continued to talk until midnight. This is no way suggests he or his friends were keeping a Sunday Sabbath!

So, why were those early believers willing to go along with the seventh day Sabbath? (I use the term "believers" rather than "Christians" because Christianity didn't come into being until after 100 CE). It's because YAHWEH said that His Sabbath was on the seventh day (Genesis 2:1-3), and He had commanded that anyone who worshipped Him was to do **exactly** as the Torah observant Hebrews:

*Numbers 15:13. **All who are native born** will do these things by this method, by presenting an offering by fire as a soothing aroma unto YHWH. 14. As for the rest in your assembly, there will be **one statute for you and the same statute for the foreigner living with you.** 15. This is an **eternal requirement throughout all your generations, that as you are so shall the foreigner be before YHWH.** 16. **The same instruction and judgment will apply equally to both you and the foreigner living with you.***

Throughout the Bible one can find absolutely no evidence that YAHWEH or Yeshua **ever** claimed the first day as holy or blessed in any way. As a matter of fact, we read that Moses told Isra'el in the wilderness on the sixth day of the week, *"Tomorrow is a holy Shabbat (Sabbath) for YAHWEH..."* (Exodus 16:23; also see Isaiah 56:2-7).

When early Gentiles accepted the Good News of Messiah Yeshua they unhesitatingly became Torah observant. History books reveal that, by the end of the First Century CE, the number of Gentile believers outnumbered Jewish believers (obviously because there were, and still are, more Gentiles in the world than Jews). But ultimately, because some Gentile believers had limited understanding of the Hebrew roots of their faith and of YAHWEH's eternal covenant with Isra'el (Romans 11:1-2), they began to veer off to form a separate religion that set in motion a "de-Judaizing process" which departed from Yeshua's original teachings.

Eventually, when Gentile Christianity emerged as the dominant faith in "Jesus," it suddenly became taboo for Jews to believe in the Torah observant Messiah Yeshua and, in order to "believe" they had to covert to the Torah-less Christianity! The time came when they were actually killed for refusing "Jesus"! Can you blame most Jews today for not wanting any part of Him? They've been driven away by the paganism that Man has incorporated into the Creator's teachings!

Even today Christians still approach Jews to admonish them that if they don't stop "being under the law" and start "believing in Jesus" (who in no way resembles the Jewish Messiah who walked upon this Earth), they are going to hell – never mind that religious Torah observant Jews ALREADY have an unparalleled relationship with YAHWEH that puts to shame any other "religious denomination"!

Back to the "Church fathers"....

Due to their limited understanding of the Jewish God and Hebrew concepts, the early "Church fathers" were extremely instrumental in changing our perception of YAHWEH and His Son. They twisted Scriptures and inserted their own opinions; changed our Savior's Name to "Jesus" (the letter J wasn't even around until the Fifteenth Century); changed his birthday from the first day of Sukkot/Feast of Tabernacles to December 25th (never mind the fact that YAHWEH never said to concentrate on His birthday at all); and they suggested He abolished YAHWEH's Torah including the seventh-day Sabbath and the Biblical Feasts, as those holy days were meant "only for Jews." (Same God, different rules? How does that make sense?) And, despite the fact that YAHWEH commanded us **not** to have idols or to make graven images of Him, they placed statues of Jesus (and Mary) in every Catholic Church and hung Him on the cross in many Christian churches! A dead man hanging on a pagan Roman death device...how can that possibly depict the Truth of God? Never mind that no one has actually seen Him face-to-face in two thousand years and is able to proclaim that today's statues are a true representation of our Savior....

As an added slap in the face of God, the Catholics and Christians decided that "the Jews" were the "bad guys" and when they weren't harassing, imprisoning or slaughtering Jews in the Inquisition, the pogroms or the Holocaust, Church leaders were teaching that Judaism had been replaced with a new religion that had new rules which, of course, in no way bore any resemblance to Judaism! How could this have been possible since Christians worshipped the same God as the Jews – the God whom the Bible describes as being the same today, yesterday and forever (Hebrews 13:8)?

Be that as it may, "Church founders" such as Ignatius (35-107 CE), Marcion (110-160 CE) and Tertullian (155-230 CE) were instrumental in tweaking the Scriptures and inserting their own opinions – which were immediately swallowed by "the world" as "true Gospel" seeking to free the Church from "false Jewish doctrines."

The following information about the early Church fathers was borrowed, with permission, from the Aramaic English New Testament:

- **Ignatius** was considered to be an "auditor" and "disciple" of John who pioneered the Greek-based Christian religion and was instrumental in the assimilation of paganism into early Christianity, packaging Christianity for a Greco-Roman Hellenic culture. Ignatius saw Jewish followers of Y'shua as nothing more than legalists and Judaizers. He despised the observance of Shabbat (Sabbath) in favor of his Ishtar (Easter) sunrise "Lord's day" Sun-Day teachings. It is scarcely possible to exaggerate the importance of the Ignatian letters to modern Christian institutions as Ignatius was a key player in the development of the modern Christian church, promoting the "infallibility of the church" and the "universal church" which had incorporated large doses of paganism. If there ever was a hierarchy loving "Christian" with a Hellenistic autocratic mindset, it was Ignatius who gave himself the nickname Theophoros (the God-bearer) and taught that deacons, presbyters and bishops were a separate category of people, high and lifted up, and infused with Jesus-like authority to be lords over people. Christians consider Ignatius as one of the all time biggest movers and shakers of the all-Gentile church. He strongly instructed that "without the bishop's supervision, no baptisms or love feasts are permitted." He also believed Mary to be the eternal virgin mother of God.

- **Tertullian:** One of Tertullian's better known "achievements" was to fall into a trance and then prophesy under the influence of the "Holy Spirit" insisting his utterances were the voice of the "Holy Spirit." While fumbling in all manner of paganism and spiritism, Tertullian picked up an "anointing" of the "Holy Ghost" and coined the word "Trinity" which is one of the most beloved doctrines of the Church to this very day (more on this in a later chapter). The "persons of the trinity" doctrine flourishes in the hierarchy-based religion which sees itself as a three-sided pyramid structure. Tertullian's works abound with puns, wit, sarcasm and a continual pounding of his opponents with invectives.

- **Marcion:** Every Christian who uses the term "Old" and "New" testament must take their hats off to Marcion as he was the one who coined these terms which perfectly reflect the Hellenistic mindset of the pagan world which is ignorant of Torah. Marcion taught that the Old and New Testaments could not be reconciled with each other, and this is what we hear in Christian churches today.

Let's examine some of the writings of these early "Church fathers" beginning with Marcion, who taught the following:

1. Moses' form of law was "eye for an eye," and that Jesus reversed this.

2. Elisha caused bears to devour the little children, but Jesus said, "let the little children come to me."

3. Joshua stopped the sun in its path to continue a slaughter of the enemy, but Paul said, "don't let the sun go down on your wrath."

4. The "Old Testament" permitted divorce and polygamy; but the "New Testament" denies both.

5. Moses enforced the Jewish Sabbath and Law, but Jesus freed believers from both.

6. God commanded that no work be done on the Sabbath, yet he told the Israelites to carry the ark around Jericho seven times on the Sabbath.

7. Graven images were prohibited by the Ten Commandments, yet Moses was instructed to fashion a bronze serpent.

8. The God of the Old Testament could not have been omniscient; otherwise he would not have asked, "Adam where are you?" (Genesis 3:9)

9. The God of the Old Testament was a ruthless God of vengeance, cruelty and wrath, but Jesus was full of grace and compassion.

10. Coined the terms "Old and New Testament."

Here are the actual Biblical meanings:

1. "Eye for eye" is an idiomatic legal term meaning to render equivalent restitution. It does not in any way suggest physical punishment of the same. The value of the eye, ear, nose or arm must be restored by the person who injured it.

2. Elisha cursed the mocking children in Name of YAHWEH. As a result 42 were torn apart by two female bears. The number 42 represents disaster towards those who turn against YAHWEH. There were 42,000 Ephraimites slain in Judges 12:6; 42 relatives of Ahaziah were killed by Jehu in 2 Kings 10:14. According to Revelation 11:2 the Gentiles wreak havoc and do all manner of blasphemy for 42 months, and because there is a connection between the number 42 and the Name of the Most High; this may be referring to the Gentiles forcing the world to bow down to their Jesus god, at pain of death. While this in itself is nothing new, YAHWEH puts a permanent

end to them by raising up His two witnesses. Elisha raised up a child from the dead and showed his great compassion for children in other places in Scripture. By viewing the Tanakh (the Jewish Bible which Christians refer to as the "Old Testament") through a Greek instead of a Hebrew mindset, Marcion, humanism and false Christianity are not judging Elisha, but YAHWEH!

Joshua would have a tough time "stopping the sun" on his own strength. Joshua 10:11-13 records how more people died when YAHWEH sent down hailstones on them, than those who Joshua's armies slew. Joshua is Yehoshua, the same name as Y'shua; he is a type of Mashiyach. Marcion and false Christianity are judging YAHWEH and overruling YAHWEH's Sovereign authority and His Word (Torah) with their own injustice system. In reality, Christians have killed more people in the name of their religion, than ancient Israelites whom YAHWEH instructed to "destroy their altars, break their images, and cut down their groves (statues)," which was so Isra'el wouldn't be tempted to sacrifice unto the pagan gods or make cast metal gods (Shemot/Exodus 34:12-17):
12. And be on your guard against making any agreement with the inhabitants of the land into which you are going, or else it will become a trap amongst you. 13. Instead, you are to tear down their altars and utterly destroy their pillars and cut down their goddess-poles [Asherim] 14. because you will not worship any other god for YHWH, Whose Name is "jealous", is a jealous elohim, 15. or else you make an agreement with the inhabitants of this land and they prostitute themselves to their gods 16. and cause your sons and daughters to also prostitute themselves to their gods. 17. You shall make for yourselves no molten god-images.

3. (Vayikra/Leviticus 20:4-5). At Petra, Jordan, archeologists have found evidence of pagan rituals where

the pagans cut the hearts out of young living children and while still beating they sacrificed them and the blood to the sun deity. That is why YAHWEH commanded them to be wiped off the face of the earth. Those who have a problem with this are willfully ignorant of the intent of YAHWEH's Commandments. But, before Mashiyach returns, YAHWEH will sanctify the Earth and establish His government. And finally, the hailstones in Joshua 10:11 remind us of Sodom and Gomorrah, which couldn't have been popular with Marcion and friends who lived in a culture where sodomy was commonplace.

4. Moshe (Moses) permitted divorce, but most Christians are ignorant of the process and consequences of obtaining release from a marriage covenant, whereas the John 8 fallacy* of the woman caught in adultery showed no consequences for adultery. In terms of polygamy YAHWEH states in D'varim/Deuteronomy 17:17 that "you shall not multiply wives." (*Verses 1-11 of John 8 do not appear in the oldest Aramaic manuscripts nor the four earliest Greek manuscripts.)

5. The Shabbat was given by YAHWEH at the Creation of the world. Mashiyach and all the *Shlichim* (apostles) observed Shabbat and brought Gentiles into the synagogues on Shabbat, to learn about the Kingdom of Elohim. The assimilation of a pagan culture into Christianity changed worship from Shabbat to Sunday.

6. We are not told that the seven days began on the first day of the week (Sunday); therefore, one cannot assume that the seventh day at Jericho was also a weekly Shabbat. The Israelites had just observed Pesach (Passover); therefore, the seven day cycle round Jericho may have started on the first day of

38

Chag haMatzah. The book of Jasher states that YAHWEH spoke to Joshua on the first day of the second month – again, this would not necessarily be on the first day of the week. Marcion's assumption is simply an attempt to judge YAHWEH's authority. YAHWEH gave the command to march, and YAHWEH pulled down the walls of Jericho. It seems Marcion had an evil imagination.

7. The bronze serpent on the pole was the antidote to the venom of the snake; those who looked to the bronze serpent were saved. Those who look to the suffering servant on the pole are saved from the bite of the serpent haSatan. Marcion willfully chose to forget that they weren't worshipping the serpent, yet he judges YAHWEH's Word and Authority as being flawed.

8. Marcion apparently couldn't appreciate that YAHWEH in His mercy gave Adam and Eve a moment to compose themselves after they had transgressed.

9. Marcion's father was a bishop of the Christian church; therefore, Marcion was simply taking more steps to define Christianity as a religion based on Hellenism.

10. By replacing the word "Covenant" with "Testament," Greek theologians tried to wrestle Jeremiah 31:31-34 away from the teachings of Y'shua and the Shlichim and divide Y'shua away from his Father YAHWEH, into their own self sustained Jesus deity.

In view of what you have just read, you can surely see that the "Church fathers" were definitely guilty of "tweaking" and/or downright twisting the Scriptures. Some would argue that, while there might have been a slight problem with semantics, it isn't really that big of a deal.

But, if it really isn't that big a deal, then perhaps we need to look at it another way: If someone were to bake a batch of homemade cookies with just a tiniest bit of cow dung mixed into the dough, would you eat them – even though there was just a smidgeon of cow dung mixed into the entire batch? Of course you wouldn't! So, why are you willing to accept misunderstanding, misinterpretation and paganism to corrupt the perfect Word of God?

Questions for Chapter 2

After reading Chapter 2 (and referring to your Bible), you should be able to answer the following questions. You may then compare your answers with those in the Appendix:

Question 1:   Please read the following scripture and then write in your own words why YAHWEH would be "tolerant" of "strange/unauthorized fire" (adding to/taking away from His rules) today: *Leviticus 10:1. But Nadav and Avihu, sons of Aaron, each took his censer and after putting fire in it also placed incense inside it and offered strange fire before YHWH, which YHWH had not commanded them to do. Then fire went out from the presence of YHWH and consumed them, and they died before YHWH.*

Question 2: Was Torah observance only for "the Jews"? Why or why not?

Question 3: Exodus 31:13 and Ezekiel 20:12 tell us that the Seventh Day Sabbath is a SIGN between God and His people. Where in the Scriptures does YAHWEH tell us to ignore the seventh day Sabbath – the day He Himself blessed and made holy (Genesis 2:1-2)?

Question 4: The Catholic "Church Fathers" are responsible for doing away with all things "Jewish" when it comes to the worship of YAHWEH; they are the reason Christians today seem to believe they are exempt from Torah. Can you name some of those "fathers" and how they twisted the Word?

Question 5: Many Catholic and Christian churches feature "Jesus hanging on a cross." In your opinion, is this right or wrong?

Question 6:   Numbers 15:13-16 shows YAHWEH reiterating four times that everyone who accepts Him is to do exactly as His Torah observant people do and that this is to be done "throughout your generations."   As a grafted-in believer in Yeshua (Romans 11:16-18), do you believe this includes you? Why or why not?

Question 7:   With whom did YAHWEH make His New Covenant?

Question 8:   What is meant by "Hebrew mindset" vs. "Greek mindset"?

Question 9:   Please read Luke 4. How did Yeshua respond to Satan's questions and comments when he tried to tempt Yeshua? From where did His quotes originate?

Question 10:   When, according to the Bible, was Yeshua born and where in the Bible are we told to celebrate His birth??

Question 11:   From your own understanding of the Bible, can **God** be born to a human being, wear diapers, be "a man of pains, well acquainted with illness" (Isaiah 53:3) or die? Why, or why not?

Question 12:   Since God cannot be born or die, how is it that "Jesus" is God, and when and where was He ever given the authority to abolish His Father's Divine Instructions to mankind (Torah)?

Chapter 3

And now, back to the Torah....

In light of the information contained within the first two chapters, can you begin to see why we need to ask the question: Why would Yeshua's death on the stake suddenly abolish YAHWEH's original Divine instructions or negate His "forever" commands?

In Biblical times the people at least had a valid excuse to "go astray": They blindly followed their rabbis because they couldn't read! But today's believers cannot make that same claim, so why are people **still** blindly following the writings of the Church fathers or their respective congregation leaders, and allowing themselves to be sent down a path that has led them completely away from Biblical Truth? Why are they not reading God's Word for themselves and speaking up when something seems "off"?

This would be a good place to ask: Have you ever wondered why there are so many and varying Christian denominations, each claiming to be "the right one"? The answer is: Because they are all adhering to just **the last third of the Bible** and ignoring YAHWEH's actual teachings! They've totally ignored the very teachings that reveal exactly who He is, how He is to be worshipped, and how we are to treat each other according to HIS desires. That's like starting toward the end a novel without bothering to understand what happened in the first two-

45

thirds. (And this refers just to Christianity; I'm not even talking about the myriad man-made "religions" that abound in the world which don't even acknowledge YAHWEH as Creator at all! They'll have their own "crosses to bear" on Judgment Day....)

Regardless, there ARE thousands of denominations and most Christians are quick to point out that Jeremiah 31 says God promised us a new covenant built on "grace" and therefore, all that is required to get into Heaven is to "believe in Jesus." The question is, since when does grace include permission to ignore YAHWEH's rules for righteousness?

In reading the "fine print" of Jeremiah 31:30 (verse 31 in some versions) we discover that the "New Covenant" was NOT made with the Gentiles nor any "religious denomination" but, rather, with the Torah observant Houses of **Isra'el** and **Yehudah** only:

Jeremiah 31:31. Behold! The day is coming, says YHWH, when I will carve out a new covenant with the house of Israel and the house of Yehudah.

Please note YAHWEH did not make a "new covenant" with the Gentiles because He did not have an "old covenant" with the Gentiles! He did, however, extend His grace and mercy to the Gentiles who, once they become believers in Yeshua, automatically become part of Isra'el!

Romans 11:16. For, if the first-fruits (are) Set Apart, then the rest of the dough (it came from is) also: and if the root is Set Apart, then also the branches. 17. And if some of the branches were plucked off; and you, an olive from the desert, were in-grafted in their place and have become an heir of the root and fatness of the olive-tree; 18. Do not boast over the branches. For if you boast, you do not sustain the root, but the root sustains you. 19. And should you say the branches were plucked off that I might be grafted into their place. 20. Very true. They were plucked off because they disbelieved; and you stand by faith. But do not be uplifted in your mind, but fear.

And God told Isra'el:

Proverbs 4:2. *"For I have given you a good teaching; do not forsake My Torah!"* (Stone Edition of the Tanakh)

The Aramaic English New Testament clears up the misconception regarding the "new covenant" in Jeremiah 31:31-34 by explaining Hebrews 8:

Hebrews 8:10. *But this is the covenant which I will give to the family of the house of Israel after those days, says Master YHWH: I will put my Torah in their minds and inscribe it on their hearts; and I will be to them an Elohim, and they shall be to me a people. 11. And one shall not teach his son of the city nor his brother, nor say: Know you Master YHWH: because they shall all know me, from the youngest of them to the oldest. 12. And I will forgive them their iniquity; and their sins will I remember no more. 13. In that he said a New (Covenant), he made the first old; and that which is old and decaying, is near to disappearing.*

The context is Jeremiah 31:31-34; what is "near to disappearing" is the sinful nature of man that breaks Torah, not the standard of Torah. Remember that **we** broke Torah, not YAHWEH. YAHWEH did not drop the standard of Torah because Israel chose disobedience; rather, He installed a Renewed Covenant to write Torah upon the heart through the work of the Ruach haKodesh, according to Mashiyach. The fact of the matter is that in Mashiyach, YAHWEH raised the bar; He magnified Torah, see Isaiah 42:21. Because mankind broke the Covenant, YAHWEH requires complete renovation on our part, not YAHWEH's part of the Covenant. This verse in its twisted form became one of the "crown jewels" of Torahless Christianity which teaches that Torah is decaying and near to disappearing, but nothing could be farther from the truth, as the following shows:

*2 Peter 3:14. Therefore, my beloved, as you expect these things, strive that you may be found by him in peace, without spot and without blemish. 15. And account the long suffering of Master YHWH to be redemption; as also our beloved brother Paul, according to the wisdom conferred on him, wrote to you; 16. as also in all his letters speaking in them of these things in which there is something difficult to be understood; (and) which they who are ignorant and unstable pervert, as they do also the rest of the Scriptures, to their own destruction. 17. You therefore, my beloved, as you know (these things) beforehand, guard yourselves or else, by going after the error of the Torahless, you fall from your steadfastness. 18. But be you **growing in grace** and in the knowledge of our Master and Redeemer Y'shua the Mashiyach and of Elohim the Father: whose is the glory now and always and to the days of eternity. Amen.*

Notice in the above that Peter writes of how Paul's letters had already been turned into a Torahless fiasco, even in Peter's day? Certainly it was not the Pharisees who were renouncing Torah Observance, but the humanist, pagan and materialist, "modernists" who operated under "Christian" labels.

It is important also, to realize that grace is the opposite of torahlessness. The Renewed Covenant prescribes Torah written upon the hearts of YAHWEH's people; therefore, when we allow Him to write Torah upon our hearts, we are receiving Torah by His Grace and entering into the Renewed Covenant.

So, what exactly is Torah?

To explain what Torah is, let's start with what it isn't:

Torah isn't legalism (man's requirements).

Torah isn't "the law" which was supposedly abolished on the cross, according to Christian understanding; but, rather, Torah comprises God's original teaching and instruction; His "do's" and "don'ts"; His blueprint for moral living. This blueprint, as mentioned earlier, is contained within the first five books of the Bible: Genesis, Exodus, Leviticus, Numbers, and Deuteronomy, also called the "Pentateuch"– and can be found in several "forever" verses, including 2 Chronicles 7:14-22 which shows that YAHWEH commanded believers to **keep His laws and rulings forever**:

2 Chronicles 7:14. "…If My people who are called out by My Name will humble themselves and seek after My Presence and turn back from their evil ways, then I will hear them from the heavens and I will pardon their sin and heal their land. 15. Then also will My eyes be open and My ears inclining attentively to the prayer that is made in this place. 16. For now I have chosen and Set-Apart this House that My Name may reside there for all eternity and My eyes and My heart be there continuously and every day. 17. And as for you, if you will walk before Me as your ancestor David walked even to do and keep all that I commanded you and keep all My statutes and ordinances, 18. then I will raise up your royal throne as I had carved it out and placed it before your ancestor David saying, You will never fail to have a descendant sit on the throne of Israel. 19. But if you turn back and set aside My statutes and commandments which I have set before you and you go after false gods and bow down to them, 20. then I will rip you out of the land that I gave them and this House that I have Set-Apart for My Name I will throw away from My Presence. I will turn it into a parable and a cutting verbal taunt among all Nations. 21. As for this House, which was brought the Great Heights everyone will be dumbstruck and say, Why has YHWH made His House and land into this [devastation]? 22. And they will say, because they abandoned YHWH, the Elohim of their ancestors Who brought them from the land of Egypt and instead they grew strong with other gods and bowed down and served them, which is why He has brought all this disaster upon them."

Today's Christians are included among the "foreigners" spoken of in Numbers 15:15-16 who love the God of Abraham, Isaac and Jacob! **You** are a part of Isra'el - Halleluyah! According to Galatians 3:27-29, believers are "one in Messiah"– "the seed of Abraham!" But yet, most have chosen to ignore (or at the very least, have forgotten, or talked themselves out of) the fact that Yeshua, the Savior YAHWEH sent to Earth as the "Word of YAHWEH in the flesh" was revealed as a Torah-observant, Sabbath and feast-keeping, kosher Jew who "walked out" Torah perfectly! (And just because Yeshua obeyed Torah does not mean He fulfilled all the prophecies. As a matter of fact, upon His return He will continue to fulfill the last three of the seven Feasts.)

Most don't seem to recognize that "fulfilled" doesn't mean "abolish or "put an end to." For instance, when you were born you fulfilled your mother's dream of having a child. Did that put an end to you? No! It means you are here and there is a purpose for you beyond "being born."

And now since you are here, you must learn some rules and regulations to make it through life safely. When your parents teach you never to stick your finger into an electrical outlet, is that instruction negated when you become an adult? Should you ever cross a busy highway without looking both ways, first, just because you no longer reside with your parents? Is it ever "okay" to bully or kill someone with whom you've had a disagreement? Of course not! Some rules are "forever." Same thing applies to your relationship with YAHWEH.

Yeshua said: *"I and the Father are one"* (John 10:30).

How much clearer could this have been stated? YAHWEH and Yeshua are ONE who are the same yesterday, today and forever (Hebrews 13:8), so why would YAHWEH have sent His Son (who was "an arm of YAHWEH, Isaiah 53:1) as a Torah observant Jew if not as an example for us to follow? Why would He have sent His Son to abolish His Divine Instructions for Righteousness? When did YAHWEH ever indicate that Torah would be "nailed to the cross" or that it was to be considered a "curse" after Yeshua's death, as most Christians today insist?

God's blueprint for holy living and behavior was not given as a temporary thing. He clearly stated that His people would be recognized by their obedience to His "forever" commands – because those permanent ordinances are what set believers apart from the rest of the world, and from pagan religions. Let's review just a few examples of some of God's "forever" statutes:

Concerning the land of Isra'el belonging to Abraham and his descendants:

Genesis 13:15. For all the land which you see, to you will I give it, and to your seed forever.....

Referencing the feast of Passover:

Exodus 12:24. And you are to preserve this instruction for you and your descendants forever.

Concerning the Biblical feasts and the seventh-day Sabbath:

Exodus 31:12. And YHWH spoke to Moshe saying, 13. "Speak to the people of Israel and say, 'You will surely keep watch and account of my Shabbats, for this is a sign between Me and you throughout all your generations, so that you will know that I am YHWH who has set you apart for Me. 14. Therefore you are to keep my Shabbat (seventh day weekly) because it is set-apart for you. Everyone who treats it as if it were a regular day must be put to death; for whoever does any work on it is to be cut away from the inward parts of his people.

51

Please note, "You will surely keep watch and account of my Shabbats," includes the Annual Shabbats, which are attached to Feast Days and count as a day of rest, no matter what day of the week they fall. Also note please note the phase, "for whoever does any work on it is to be cut away from the inward parts of his people": This is not just a casual removal being expressed here but a brutal ripping away of the offender from everyone he knows and loves.

Leviticus 23:2. Speak to the people of Israel: These are My Mo'edim--the appointed times of YHWH which you are to proclaim as Set-Apart occasions.

Again: Who are "the people of Isra'el"? Anyone who follows the God of Abraham, Isaac, and Jacob! It cannot be emphasized enough that, as a grafted in Christian believer YOU are to be Torah-obedient, YOU are to eat kosher, and YOU are to keep the seventh day Sabbath and the Biblical feasts – all of which foreshadow Yeshua!

*Exodus 31:16. So the people of Israel are keep watch over and preserve the Shabbat, to **maintain the Shabbat throughout all their generations as a perpetual covenant. 17. It is a sign between Me and the people of Israel for all eternity,** for in six days YHWH made the heavens and the earth, but on the seventh day He completed His work and rested.'"*

In verse 17 above, note that the point of view has switched from YAHWEH talking to Moshe and telling him what to say, to Moshe summarizing those comments here because YAHWEH calls Himself "I AM" and not "He is". In many other places though YAHWEH will say, "I, YAHWEH" which to mankind is His Name but to Himself it is "I, He Who Is, say to you…"

Please note, the Sabbath is a **sign** of Yahweh, His seal which represents His authority as Creator. It is what will separate "us believers" from all those who are atheists or who serve other gods!

Those who have the seal or "Mark of God" (Genesis 4:15, Ezekiel 9:4, Ezekiel 9:6, John 6:27, 2 Corinthians 1:2, Ephesians 1: 13, Ephesians 4:30, 2 Timothy 2:19) are the ones who not only have the testimony of our Messiah, but they are also Torah-observant (Revelation 12:17 and 14:12) as was Yeshua who Himself kept kosher and observed the seventh-day Sabbath and the feasts, etc.

*Revelation 12:17. – "The dragon was infuriated over the woman and went off to fight the rest of her children, those who obey God's commands **and** bear witness to Yeshua."*

*Revelation 14:12. Here is the patience of the Set Apart believers who keep the commandments of Elohim, **and** the faith of Y'shua.*

"Yeshua's faithfulness" included the fact that He was completely Torah observant – and He **never** suggested we could toss Torah out the window after His death! Now, who are those who obey God's commands **and** bear witness to Yeshua? Certainly not those who refuse to adhere to Torah! The "commands" refer not just to the Ten Commandments but to all of YAHWEH's commands, without which we would be no better than the "heathens"....

We must always remember that YAHWEH continuously warned Israel not to follow the Gentile nations and their heathen ways:

*Deuteronomy 18:9. "When you enter the land that YHWH your Elohim is giving you, **do not** learn to imitate the depraved customs of those nations. 10. **No one among you** is to make his son or daughter pass through fire. Further, **no one among you** may practice divination or sorcery or cast spells or tell fortunes. 11. **No one among you** is allowed to consult a medium or a familiar spirit or ask questions of the dead. 12. **Everyone who does these things** is an* *abomination to YHWH and YHWH your Elohim is driving out the inhabitants of those nations because of these abominations that they are doing. 13. You must be wholehearted with YHWH your Elohim. 14. For these nations, which you will dispossess, practice divination and sorcery; but you, YHWH your Elohim does not allow this among you."*

The "Replacement Theology" excuse...

Using certain misunderstood/misinterpreted verses as "proof" that the Jews were cursed and are no longer God's Chosen, some Christians insist that "the church" has replaced Isra'el and they are therefore not required to adhere to Old Testament teachings. For instance:

Matthew 27:25. And answered all the people and said, "Let his blood be upon us and upon our children."

Does the above mean there is a blood curse upon the Jews? No! First, Exodus 20:4 is being referenced here, which indicates that YAHWEH visits sins up to the fourth generation. Some of the Sanhedrin were concerned that Yeshua was innocent; they concluded that if he was innocent, a worst case scenario would bring a curse on them lasting four generations. However, if Yeshua was guilty and if the Romans became angry, they feared Israel would be wiped off the face of the earth; hence not only four generations but all future generations would be affected. This idea was also stated by the high priest in John 11:48. This grossly misunderstood (or twisted) verse was fashioned into a "the blood curse" by Christians against the Jewish people.

"Replacement theology" seems to be rampant in some of our modern Christian churches. But, what does the Bible say about this?

Moshe (Moses) told the people of Isra'el:

Deuteronomy 7:6. For you are a people Set-Apart for YHWH your Elohim. YHWH your Elohim has selected you from all the peoples of the earth to be His own precious treasured possession. 7. It was not you were the most numerous of all the nations that YHWH set His heart towards you and chose you. Quite the opposite—since you were the smallest of all the peoples! 8. Rather, because YHWH loved you and kept account of His oath which He swore to your ancestors, YHWH then brought you out with a strong hand and redeemed you from the house of bondage from under the hand of Pharaoh, ruler of Egypt.

NOTE: In Hebraic thought every major good or bad part of life has a "house" that we are said to reside in. So we have a "house" of life, a "house" of wickedness and, in this case, a house of bondage and a house of freedom.

The prophet Jeremiah wrote:

*Jeremiah 31:37. (36 in some versions) Thus says YHWH: If the high heavens can be measured and the foundations searched from below, then I will also cast off the **descendants of Israel** for all that they have done, thus says YHWH.*

And from the prophet Isaiah:

*Isaiah 66:22. For just like the new heavens and the new earth that I am making will endure before My face, so too will **your descendants and your name** endure. 23. From New Moon (month) to New Moon and from Shabbat to Shabbat, all humanity will come and bow down before Me, says YHWH.*

In other words, **no one** has replaced the descendants of Israel (Jews) as YAHWEH's "chosen" and YAHWEH never changed His "forever" commands to fit into the theology of today's modern Christians. Christians, for the most part, have taken the God of Abraham, Isaac and Jacob, and turned Him into someone unrecognizable. In many cases, He's depicted as a blue-eyed, long-haired, blond "Adonis" instead of the tallit wearing, Sabbath-keeping, Torah observant Jew that He was.

In the allegory of the Olive Tree in Romans 11, Rav Sha'ul (the Apostle Paul) said that the root of the Olive Tree (Isra'el) was holy and that the Gentiles, through the atoning death of Messiah Yeshua, were grafted in and could therefore partake of the nourishing sap from the olive root. He also warned that they shouldn't feel superior because they were not the original holy root; rather, they were "grafted in" branches which could be cut off just as easily as the natural branches.

Being "grafted in" does not in any way mean Christians have "replaced" the Jewish people! There are no "Christian denominations" in YAHWEH's Kingdom; there is only Isra'el! The grafting in is a great privilege which requires you to realize you are set apart for Him (Romans 12:1). And along with the privilege comes the responsibility of obeying His "forever" commands....

Deuteronomy 5:29. How I would earnestly wish for their innermost beings to remain as they are now forever; that they would understand My majesty and obey all of My Mitzvot (Commandments), so that all may be pleasant for them and their children forever!

Ezekiel 20:11. I gave them My statutes and showed them My ordinances, through which if a person obeys them he will have life through them. 12. I gave them My Shabbats to be a sign between Me and them, so that they would know that I, YHWH, am the One Who makes them Set-Apart.

Questions for Chapter 3

After reading Chapter 3 (and referring to your Bible), you should be able to answer the following questions. You may then compare your answers with those in the Appendix:

Question 1: The Bible in several places states that YAHWEH's Word is forever. Can you explain why Yeshua's death on the stake would suddenly abolish YAHWEH's original Divine instructions or negate His "forever" commands? Did "forever" end at the beginning of the "New Testament"?

Question 2: Can you find any evidence anywhere in the Bible where YAHWEH ever dropped His Standards for Torah, just because the human race was disobedient? If so, please write the pertinent scripture references here:

Question 3: YAHWEH has endless patience with those who are trying their best to obey His Commands, but He removes His Hand and His Grace from those who refuse to follow Him (as was the case with Pharaoh). Still, many are quick to point out that we no longer have to bother with Torah because we are no longer under the law but, rather, under grace. When and where in the Bible do you think "grace" began, and did it give us permission to ignore God's rules?

Question 4: John 17:3 informs us that eternal life is knowing God and knowing Yeshua. Is there any way outside of Torah that we can possibly "know God." If so, how?

Question 5: According to Jeremiah 31:30-32, with whom did YAHWEH make His "new covenant" and how does if affect you?

Question 6: John 10:30 says: *I and the Father are one.* Hebrews 13:8 tells us YAHWEH is the same yesterday, today and forever. So, why would He have sent His Son?

Question 7: When did YAHWEH ever indicate that Torah would be "nailed to the cross" or that it was to be considered a "curse" after Yeshua's death, as most Christians today insist?

Question 8:   As grafted in believers, Gentiles are part of Israel, and as such, do you believe YAHWEH would treat His "adopted children" any differently from His "natural" ones? Why or why not?

Question 9: Who are "the people of Isra'el"?

Question 10: Please study the following scriptures and explain who the people are who obey God's commands AND bear witness to Yeshua:

*Revelation 12:17. And the dragon was enraged against the woman; and he went to make war upon the remnant of her seed who keep the Commandments of Elohim **and** have the testimony of Y'shua.*

*Revelation 14:12. Here is the patience of the Set Apart believers who keep the commandments of Elohim, **and** the faith of Y'shua.*

Question 11: In Revelation 12:17, at whom is the Dragon enraged?

Question 12: What does it mean to OBEY God? What, exactly, are you as a Christian, obeying?

Question 13: Throughout the Bible we can see that YAHWEH's covenants, although modified according to His will, were never negated, abolished or replaced. What, exactly, changed when we received the "New Covenant"?

Question 14: YAHWEH considers His Seventh Day Sabbath a SIGN between Him and His people (Exodus 31:16-17). That being the case, please cite any scripture that tells us where His Sabbath (day of rest) was changed to the "first day."

Chapter 4

Torah was around in "the beginning"....   Notes:

Returning to our discussion of Torah – Torah goes all the way back to the Garden of Eden when YAHWEH gave Adam and Eve one simple command, which was to stay away from the Tree of the Knowledge of Good and Evil:

Genesis 2:16. And YHWH Elohim commanded the man, saying, Of every tree of the garden you may freely eat: 17. but of the tree of the knowledge of good and evil, you shall not eat of it: for in the day that that you eat of it you shall surely die.

YAHWEH couldn't have made it any clearer: With one exception, Adam and Eve were allowed to eat from every tree in the Garden, including from the "tree of life" (Genesis 2:9). Eating the fruit of the tree of the knowledge of good and evil, however, meant death (note God didn't say "immediate physical death," but "certain" death). Had Adam and Eve chosen to obey God instead of allowing themselves to be deceived by Satan, things would surely have turned out differently for mankind!

Regardless, here we have the first indication that breaking YAHWEH's Torah commands is a lethal act – an act that requires an animal/blood sacrifice. Please note that, in Genesis 3:21 we have the earliest known animal sin sacrifice because, the first thing YAHWEH did immediately after confronting Adam and Eve about their transgression, was to cover them with the skin of an innocent animal, killed just for them – an animal they had surely known and named!

Shortly after their eviction from the Garden of Eden for disobedience, we are shown the struggles of mankind, beginning with the story of how Cain killed Abel in a jealous rage concerning their sin sacrifice offerings:

Genesis 4:2. And again she gave birth to his brother Abel. And Abel was a keeper of sheep, but Cain was a tiller of the ground. 3. And in process of time it came to pass, that Cain brought of the fruit of the ground an offering to YHWH. 4. And Abel, he also brought of the firstlings of his flock and their fat. And YHWH had respect to Abel and to his offering: 5. but to Cain and to his offering he had not respect. And Cain was very angry, and his countenance fell. 6. And YHWH said to Cain, Why are you angry? And why is your countenance fallen? 7. If you do well, shall it not be lifted up? And if you do not do well, sin crouches at the door: and to you shall be its desire, but you can rule over it.

At this point, one might question: How did Cain and Abel know they were to give sin offerings to YAHWEH? Why did the Creator accept Abel's offering and not Cain's? Did He make up new rules on the spur of the moment? No! The above is evidence that Cain and Abel already knew "right from wrong" – taught to them, no doubt, by their parents who had "the law" laid down to them by YAHWEH Himself; and they knew the rules about certain sacrifices. The whole scenario is proof that Torah – God's Instruction in Righteousness – was clearly around since the beginning! These instructions included atonement for sin:

Hebrews 9:22. ...because everything, according to Torah, is purified with blood: and without the shedding of blood there is no forgiveness of sin.

Although the Bible doesn't tell us exactly where and how YAHWEH showed His creation the proper way to offer sin sacrifices, the fact remains that the command was passed down at some point; and it continued from one generation to the next – until the day our Savior was crucified; thus, forever abolishing the need for sin sacrifices.

It is imperative, however, to remember that our relationship with God did not end just because Man was prone to sin. Man ultimately suffered the consequences of disobedience – a death sentence – which changed the relationship with YAHWEH but did not put an end to it, thanks to His patience, grace and mercy.

Noah (who was not a "Jew") knew Torah....

Romans 6:23 tells us, the ultimate consequence of sin is death. In Noah's time, the whole Earth was wiped out because there was a complete rejection of Torah and evil reigned. The flood served as the ultimate warning to mankind that, although our Creator was patient and merciful, He would NOT condone willful sinning.

As we journey through the "Old Testament" we see that YAHWEH offered His creation chance after chance to get themselves "right" with Him; but mankind kept failing. During the time of the flood, only Noah and his family were saved because Noah was "righteous" (Genesis 7:1). During this time YAHWEH kept escalating His teachings as evidenced in Genesis 9:1-17 which outlines the new covenant He made with Noah and his sons; and from this we can also see that the Earth's steady population growth necessitated more rules and regulations to keep the people in check.

Before we go on, have you ever noticed that in Genesis 7:2-15 God told Noah to take both "clean" and "unclean" animals onto the ark, and that Noah offered only "clean" birds and animals on the altar after he left the ark (Genesis 8:20)? The difference between "clean and unclean" was not actually clarified until the time of the Exodus, but at least we can see that the idea of kosher eating and "proper" sacrifices was already around well before Moses, as we saw in the case of the sacrifices presented by Cain and Abel.

Genesis 9 goes on to tell us that the whole Earth was populated by the three sons of Noah: Shem, Ham and Japheth. It is important to note here, that *neither Noah nor his sons were Hebrews or Jews! Neither were Cain and Abel or even Adam and Eve – but yet they were ALL Torah observant!* (The term "Hebrew" was first associated with Abram and his sons [beginning in Genesis 12], whom YAHWEH identified as "Hebrews," chosen to make known His mighty Name and to ultimately bring salvation to the world. "Jews" however, were not around until after Jacob and his wife Leah gave birth to their son Yehudah [Judah – the tribe from which Yeshua came; see Genesis 29:35 and 49:10] where the term "Jew" originated and ultimately became a blanket term for Israelites.)

We have seen that from Adam's time on, man has known about YAHWEH's demand for obedience, the need for blood sacrifices to atone for sin and about "clean" and "unclean" animals; and, consequently, Christian church leaders have no leg to stand on when they insist that believing Gentiles don't need to be Torah observant because "those old rules applied only to the Jews"…

Abraham, Isaac and Jacob (who were not "Jews") also knew and obeyed Torah....

As the Bible shows, YAHWEH continuously revealed Himself to Man, always precisely outlining His divine desires. He never forced new or irrational ideas on Man; rather, He expanded on the **same principles** that ultimately comprised the Ten Commandments (Exodus 34:28) which were presented to Moshe (Moses). Let's briefly discuss what happened on Mt. Sinai:

Exodus 19:3. And Moshe went up to Elohim and YHWH called to him from the mountain: "This is what you will say to the household of Ya'akov, and proclaim to the people of Israel: 4. 'You have seen yourselves what I have made happen to the Egyptians, and how I carried you up on the wings of eagles and brought you near to Me. 5. Now, if you will pay special attention and hear My voice and hold fast to My covenant, then you will be My own possession from among all the peoples 6. and you will be a kingdom of Cohanim [priests] unto Me and a Set-Apart nation." These are the words that you shall speak to the people of Israel.

Exodus goes on (verses 19:8 and 24:3) to reveal that Isra'el accepted YAHWEH's offer, which formed the beginning of the Mosaic covenant. Remember, Isra'el consisted of "a mixed crowd" who accompanied Moshe out of Egypt (Exodus 12:38). It cannot be reiterated enough that Isra'el includes not only the Hebrews/Jews but **anyone** who accepts the God of Abraham, Isaac and Jacob (Exodus 12:49 and Numbers 9:14) who is the "same yesterday, today and forever" (Hebrews 13:8). One God, one set of rules! We're all equal in His eyes….

Keeping in mind what you've learned thus far, the question begs to be asked again: Does it make any sense at all that Yeshua would have "nailed" the entire Torah to the cross"?

Divine Law and the priesthood

As we've seen, Divine Law and priesthood have always been around, as far back as Adam and Eve. Once Man had partaken from tree of the knowledge of good and evil, he and his offspring were destined to reap the consequences; and these consequences required sacrifices and offerings to God….

The sacrifice for sin was always the shedding of innocent blood. Why blood? Because blood is our life force; without it, we die. Why an innocent animal? Apparently, to make man feel the anguish over the loss of an innocent life on his behalf! Something had to die so that we sinners could continue living in God's Presence!

While Adam's children were busy procreating and populating the Earth a high priest was not yet required to perform the sacrifices and so, in those days, every man offered his own sacrifice and acted as his own priest (as in the cases of Abel, Noah, Melchizedek, Job and Abraham).

The need for a high priest – an intercessor between God and man – arose when Isra'el's population began to grow. The priesthood was made up of one High Priest along with many other "regular" priests. The High Priest represented Isra'el as a whole nation before YAHWEH, while the "regular" priests represented individual Israelites. (Duties of the high priest are outlined in the books of Exodus and Leviticus, see for example Exodus 28:6-42; 29:6; 39:27-29; and Leviticus 6:19-23 and 21:10.)

Yeshua haMashiyach, who came to Earth in the form of a Man, ultimately became our High Priest. Yeshua chose to offer Himself on our behalf and bore the sins of all of us permanently – and the only thing required of us, in return, was to "believe" in His shed blood at the cross as our Final Sin Sacrifice, which allowed us to become "new creatures in Christ" who desire to follow **all** God's commandments (Hebrews 3:1; John 3:15-18; 1 Peter 1:18-19; John 10:8-9; John 10:10; 2 Cor. 5:17-18; Matthew 1:21; Isaiah 7:14).

In a nutshell, what changed?

Throughout the Bible we can see that YAHWEH's covenants, although modified according to His will, were never negated, abolished or replaced. For instance, let's examine what happened when we received the "New Covenant":

The *covenant* changed, but the following did NOT:

- Torah
- YAHWEH's provisions
- The penalty for disobedience
- YAHWEH's promises

What DID change?

The Steward: Yeshua, as the Word of YAHWEH in the flesh (not "incarnate" because that denotes God died!), is now the standard bearer. Moses is no longer the steward, thereby fulfilling the prophecy of **Deuteronomy 18:***18. I will raise up for them a prophet like you from among their kinsmen. I will put my words in his mouth, and he will tell them everything I order him. 19. Whoever doesn't listen to my words, which he will speak in my name, will have to account for himself to me.*

The Torah is administered (not replaced) under a new covenant – It is now written on our hearts via the Spirit of YAHWEH, and not on clay tablets alone, thus fulfilling the prophecy of **Jeremiah 31:***31. Behold! The day is coming, says YHWH, when I will carve out a new covenant with the house of Israel and the house of Yehudah. 32. It will not be like the covenant I made with their ancestors in the day when I took them by the hand and brought them out of the land of Egypt, because the broke My covenant even though I was a husband to them, says YHWH. 33. But this is the covenant I will carve out with the house of Israel after those days. Proclaims YHWH: I will put My Torah-instruction deep within them and within their innermost being will I write it. And I will be their Elohim and they shall be My people. 34. No longer will everyone teach their neighbor to know YHWH for they will all know Me, from the least of them to the greatest of them. (And) YHWH has spoken: For I will forgive their depravity and remember their sin no more. 35. And YHWH also says: Who gives the sun for a light by day and the ordinances of the moon and of the stars as a light for the night? Who divides and stirs* *up the sea into thunderous waves? YHWH Tsavaot {of Hosts} is His Name!*

Again, please note that YAHWEH made His "New Covenant" **not** with the Gentiles, or the Christians or the Muslims or anyone except for the Houses of Israel and Yehudah.

Also, please note that many who believe "Torah is now written on our hearts" are under the erroneous assumption that they don't have to do anything but "believe in Jesus." What this actually means, however, is that we are willing to follow YAHWEH's instruction and learn and obey Torah; NOT that we are born with an innate knowledge about His teachings and commands which we can ignore at will!

The priesthood has changed. Instead of an Aaronic high priest, the high priest is Yeshua – fulfilling the prophecy of Psalms 110, where King David writes: *1. YHWH says to my human master: Sit at My right hand, until I set your enemies before you like a footstool for your feet. 2. YHWH will stretch your mighty scepter from Zion saying: Have dominion in the midst of all your enemies. Your people will come forward willingly 3. on that day of Your power, in Set-Apart splendor, from the womb of the dawn! Yours was the dew of youth. 4. YHWH has sworn it and He will never go back on His Word: You are a Cohen (Priest) forever in the same manner as Malki-Tzedek!*

The sacrificial system has changed. Under the original covenant, animal sacrifices were offered. Under the new covenant, Messiah Himself is the sacrifice. This fulfills the foreshadowing of Psalm 40, relating to animal sacrifice because he chose to martyr Himself on our behalf: *6. You have given me understanding that sacrifices and grain offerings are not Your desire and sin offerings are not what You have asked of us. 7. So then I said, Behold! I am coming and will bring a scroll of a book that is written about what has happened to me. 8. It is my great joy to do what is pleasant to You my Elohim; and Your Torah-instruction in the very core of my innermost being.*

Taken together, the new covenant still requires a sacrifice, a high priest to mediate on our behalf, an altar, and a sanctuary. The roles, however, are now filled by Yeshua, as He is all these things.

Ultimately, as you know, YAHWEH made **us** priests to stand and minister in His Name (I Peter 2:5, 2:9, Revelation 1:6, 5:9-10)!   But, we can only do this if we are willing to follow ALL of His "forever" commands; we don't have the right to pick and choose or change any of His divine commands!   YAHWEH **never** changed His mind about obedience to Torah or about the punishment for the consequences of sin.

What you've read so far has broadly outlined the history of God's people before the actual giving of the Torah through Moses, which showed that Man always had a relationship with God.   YAHWEH's goal wasn't to impose a myriad hard-to-follow rules on us! His desire for us was to have a blueprint for moral, Godly living which would allow us to continue having a relationship with Him.

(By the way, examples of YAHWEH's commandments are sprinkled throughout the Torah. See Genesis 26:2-5; Exodus 15:25-27; chapter 16; 20:6; Leviticus chapters 22, 26, 27; Numbers chapters 15, 36; Deuteronomy chapters 4, 5, 6, 7, 8, 10, 11, 13, 26, 27, 28, 30, 31. There are more, but you get the picture: God was very adamant about people following **all** His teachings because they were for our own good.)

We also need to remember that, just because Moses was the first one to present God's teachings as "Torah," YAHWEH - not Moses - is the Creator of the Torah. YAHWEH shared some of His wisdom with Moses, who was to pass it on to the Hebrews and to those who chose to follow the God of Abraham, Isaac and Jacob.

Are you beginning to see why Y AHWEH said His Torah would stand forever (2 Chronicles 7:14-22)? How could something that is so good for us ever be considered a "curse" (as the Christian church keeps insisting)?

As you know, in our fallen state, it is impossible to please God. Unless we have placed our faith and trust in Messiah Yeshua, our Final Sin Sacrifice, we have no other way to obtain eternal life. However, that does not make Torah the "curse of the law"– rather, "the curse" is our endeavor to acquire salvation by following the law without faith because, as mere human beings with limited human mindsets, we are prone to stumble at some point:

James 2:8. And if in this you fulfill the Torah of Elohim, as it is written, You will love your neighbor as yourself, you will do well: 9. but if you have partiality towards persons, you commit sin; and you are convicted by Torah as breakers of Torah. 10. For he that will keep the whole Torah and yet fail in one aspect of it, is an enemy to the whole Torah. 11. For he who said, "You will not commit adultery," said also, "You will not kill." If then you commit no adultery, but you do murder, you have become a defiler of Torah. 12. So speak and so act as persons that are to be judged by the Torah of perfect freedom. 13. For judgment without mercy will be on him who has practiced no mercy: by mercy, you will be raised above judgment.

What will the people be judged by (verse 12)? **Torah!** Y AHWEH wasn't "cursing" man when He gave us some guidelines to live by. ALL of His commandments were given for a reason. ALL of His commandments taught man right from wrong, and how to obey God and to worship Him properly. Mashiyach (Messiah) redeemed us from the "curse of the Torah," by becoming accursed.

The "Curse of the Torah" by the way, is found in Deuteronomy 27:15-26. There are 12 specific curses mentioned; however, one can also apply this to the entire Torah. If anyone knowingly or unknowingly sins, but does not seek forgiveness and restitution, they are under the curse. There is a "Y" in the road of every choice we make: one road leads to blessing, the other to a curse.

Yeshua was "accursed" by his accusers, but Christians who insist on following man's opinions instead of God's Word, sadly teach that YAHWEH and Torah accused Yeshua. However, Yeshua was the Perfect Lamb who never broke Torah; therefore, could never come under any curse of Torah. We come under the curse when we sin and refuse to turn to YAHWEH!

It's time the world became aware of the fact that YAHWEH handed down many more requirements besides just the Ten Commandments, and that He never, ever said to disregard His Torah. Yeshua came to establish and confirm Torah, and also to expose the man-made opinions and traditions that had become entangled in God's teachings. Paul verified this when he said: *Do, we then nullify Torah by faith? May it never be! On the contrary, we establish Torah.* (Romans 3:31).

Questions for Chapter 4

After reading Chapter 4 (and referring to your Bible), you should be able to answer the following questions. You may then compare your answers with those in the Appendix:

Question 1: When were the first known Torah commands originally given?

Question 2: What does the forgiveness of sin require?

Question 3: When was the first known sin sacrifice performed?

Question 4: When did the last known sin sacrifice occur?

Question 5: What is the ultimate consequence of sin?

Question 6: When did YAHWEH start doling out "grace" and who were the recipients?

Question 7: How do we know Cain and Abel were Torah observant?

Question 8: How do we know Noah was Torah observant?

Question 9: Were any of the following "Jews"? Adam, Eve, Cain, Abel, Noah? (Think about how many generations passed [Abraham, Isaac and Jacob!] before "Jews" came onto the scene – and yet every believer up until then was already Torah observant!)

Question 10: Genesis 7:2-15 tell us that Noah was commanded to take both "clean" and "unclean" animals onto the ark with him. In your own words, why do you suppose that was?

Question 11: Exodus 12:38 tells us Isra'el consisted of "a mixed crowd" accompanying Moshe out of Egypt. Exodus 19:8 and 24:3 show that Isra'el accepted YAHWEH's offer to obey His "every word." What is the significance of these statements?

Question 12: Many who sin are quick to cry, "You're judging me!" when someone attempts to tell them to stop sinning. The Bible, however, commands us to correct sinners (Titus 1:13, 2 Tim. 2:15, etc.), and James 2:12 tells us that _____, not man's opinions, are one's judge. It is NOT "judging" when we weigh someone's actions against what _____ says.

Question 13: If the Torah was "abolished" and the "Old Testament" doesn't pertain to today's believers, why are Christian pastors still teaching the Ten Commandments or telling church members to tithe?

Question 14: Was Torah just for "the Jews"? Why or why not?

Question 15: What conditions changed when YAHWEH made a "new covenant" with the Houses of Israel and Judah?

Chapter 5

The misunderstood, misinterpreted writings of Paul   Notes:

Yeshua attempted to make people realize that He had not come to abolish Torah but, rather, the man-made traditions and the teachings of some of the rabbis who had twisted the Words of YAHWEH. But, as has always been the case, Man wasn't listening then, and he isn't listening now because we are **still** misinterpreting the Word of God! Example:

Matthew 26:34. Y'shua said to him, Truly I say to you, that in this night before the cock crows you will deny me three times.

Many, if not most pastors have interpreted this to mean a literal rooster. I once listened to a whole sermon where the pastor spoke about how "the rooster" was the only one who was doing God's will that morning. Had this pastor been familiar with Hebrew or Aramaic, he would have been surprised to discover that this passage referred to the "temple crier" – a *Gaver*, Hebrew for "cock" or "rooster," a person responsible for opening the temple before dawn and calling out loudly two or three times to announce the early morning services....

This type of misinterpretation is also true for the much-misunderstood teachings of Rav Sha'ul (Apostle Paul) whose teachings are constantly used by Christians to prove that "the law is a curse and it was nailed to the cross." To wit:

Colossians 2:14. ...and, by his mandates, he blotted out the handwriting of our debts which (handwriting) existed against us, and took (it) from the midst and affixed (it) to his stake. 15. And, by yielding up his body, he showed contempt for principalities and authorities; and put them to shame, openly, in his own person.

Please note Yeshua wiped away the **bill of charges** (sins) against us, not Torah! Verse 15 goes on to explain what Yeshua nailed to the cross was **not** Torah but rather the man-made laws! The same person who wrote that the Torah is holy just and good could not possibly be referring to the **Torah** as the "certificate of debt" or "bill of charges"! Let's study this a little further:

Referring once more to author and Aramaic scholar Andrew Gabriel Roth, none of the words that mean "Torah" appear in either the Greek or the Aramaic version of Colossians 2:14. This means "Torah" is not inferred, because "Torah" never appears! Roth writes:

> "So what then is 'the certificate of debt'? In the original texts the Aramaic word *khawbayn* means both 'debt' and 'sin'. In addition, Y'shua used the same word in the Sermon on the Mount when he says, *'Forgive our debts/offenses, as we forgive those who are in debt to us/have offended us.'* Interesting to note, half the Greek texts read 'debt' and the other half 'offense' because each group chose one of this word's two meanings.

> "However, in Aramaic thought, to be in sin is literally to be in debt! Note also that *khawbayn* is in the plural state, meaning 'the certificate of our debts', as in humanity collectively. That is why Y'shua says else-where:

> *"Y'shua said to them, 'If you were blind you would have no sin, but since you say 'we see', your sin/debt remains.'"*

And so, the certificate of our debts is simply a record of all the transgressions that we have generated throughout our lives. The Torah tells us what those sins are, but what Y'shua did was to take the transcript of those sins and nail those to the cross!

"So when we are guilty of sin, YAHWEH is one witness to that guilt, and the record that is generated of that sin is another. However, with the reconcilement of Y'shua on the cross dying in our place, that second witness/record against us is obliterated, and the Torah remains simply to guide us in the path of righteousness for the rest of our redeemed lives."

As you can see, it is very important to know what the original texts state....

At this point it must be mentioned that people today are viewing Paul's writings through a "Greek" as opposed to a Hebrew mindset. If his teachings were being viewed as he had intended, there would be a lot less confusion. After all, why would any God-fearing, obedient believer desire to perpetuate the idea that YAHWEH would allow Yeshua to nail to the cross the **only** divine blueprint for moral behavior? What possessed us to think we could **dare** view His original teachings as a "curse"?

We need to give Paul, the emissary to the Gentiles, some credit because, unless one is bilingual or has studied a foreign language, they will find it hard to fathom the frustration he must have experienced in trying to convey the complicated messages of the Hebrew language into Greek (which also begs the question: Why would the Apostles who spoke Hebrew and Aramaic, have written the Gospels in Greek?)....

Be that as it may, a thorough study of Paul's writings read in context reveals that he **never** went against Yeshua's teachings, nor did he ever renounce the Torah – although many Christians like to cite text from places such as Galatians 2:3-16 as "proof" that he did. Unless one is viewing Paul's writings through a "Hebrew mindset," these verses seem to show that he suggests Gentiles don't need to be circumcised; but nothing could be further from the truth, as explained in a footnote on Galatians 2 in the Aramaic English New Testament:

> Unlike the contemporary traditions of Judaism in Paul's day, a soul who follows Mashiyach is not immediately forced to be circumcised once they show interest, as this is something that is done according to the intent of a person's heart. Circumcision is a voluntary choice, just as it would also be unthinkable to force someone to be immersed (baptized). Every soul must willfully volunteer to fulfill their obligations as their soul is being matured by the Ruach haKodesh. Paul clearly indicates that the requirement for circumcision has in NO way been negated. Circumcision is a demonstration of Faith and Obedience when a person does so according to the leading of the Ruach haKodesh (Holy Spirit), but NOT on the basis of social, peer, or status quo pressure.

Furthermore, a comparison between Galatians 2 and Romans 2:13-14 reveals that Paul, in fact, is NOT speaking against the Torah at all:

Romans 2:13. For not the hearers of Torah are righteous before Elohim; but the doers of Torah are being made righteous.

Again, here is a footnote from the AENT:

> (Ref. Romans 2:13) Notice how those "under Torah" and those "doers of Torah" are put in opposition to one another; therefore, both cannot simultaneously be in error. This is clarified with the phrase "for doers of

Torah will be made righteous." So, if Torah-doers are made righteous, it stands to reason Torah itself is NOT passing away! The fact that such deep pro-Torah statements are being sent to Gentiles in Rome speaks volumes of how mainstream Christianity is perverting Rav Shaul's teachings. "Under Torah" means to look to its rituals as a form of magic; a power that needs no purity of intent to bring about blessing, but merely fixed repetition. Torah in itself provides no authority of magic rather, Torah has authority because it is YAHWEH's instruction to man! So "under Torah" is a false teaching that has never been true according to the Tanakh ("Old Testament"): YAHWEH blesses man for Torah observance, which is obedience to His Commandments. Notice in Matthew 15 how Y'shua rebukes the Pharisees on this very issue, how they set aside YAHWEH's Torah (instructions) in favor of their traditions.

(Ref. Romans 2:14, Rav Shaul does not suggest that Gentiles are spontaneously mastering Torah. The point is they should learn the written Torah without distraction from Pharisaic traditions which are not rooted in the plain understanding of Torah.)

Moving on, Acts 21:15-21, which was written after Paul wrote the Galatians, clearly reveals that he was Torah observant, and that his teachings (especially the misconception in Romans 8 that, "if someone is led by the Spirit, they are not under law..." and Galatians 3 that "the law is a curse") have been severely misunderstood because Paul was referring not to Torah but to **man's** law/ legalism.

Since we're discussing Galatians...

Many Christians attempt to use Galatians 3 to show that "the law is a curse"; never stopping to wonder why or how

God's Instructions in Righteousness could ever be considered bad! Without His Torah, we would have no blueprint for moral, holy living, so what would make His laws a "curse"?

But that is exactly what is being taught in Christian churches!

The problem stems from the misinterpretation of Paul. It is as simple as that, but Paul, in his letter to the Galatians, is very hard to understand. In fact, many a scholar has argued that a true understanding of Paul's arguments in Galatians follows only from a line-by-line dissection of his text. And one cannot fully understand Paul unless, at the same time, you possess a detailed knowledge of the Tanach. Example:

*Galatians 3:10. For those who are servants of Torah are still under a curse, for it is written, "Cursed is everyone who does not act on all that is written in this book of Torah." 11. But that no man is made righteous by Torah before Elohim is evident, for it is written, "the righteous will live by faith". 12. Thus Torah is not made by faith, but whosoever will do the things that are written in it, will live in it. 13. **But Mashiyach has redeemed us from the "curse of Torah," by becoming accursed for us, for it is written: "Cursed is everyone who hangs on a tree".***

So what, exactly is Paul trying to say? There are 12 specific curses mentioned in Deuteronomy 27:15-26 and in Galatians 3:10, Paul mentioned Deuteronomy 27:26. So is Paul suggesting that "Torah" is a curse? He is not, and would not, because Paul knows exactly what "the curse of Torah" is! It is found in Deuteronomy 11:26-28:

Deuteronomy 11:26. See, I am placing before you this very day a blessing and a curse. 27. For the blessing, if you hear and (shema) do the Mitzvot (Commandments) of YHWH your Elohim that I am commanding you today. 28. For the curse, if you do not hear and do the Mitzvot of YHWH your Elohim and instead turn aside from the path that I am directing you to today and then choose to follow other gods that you have not known.

NOTE: Hebrew *shema* has always had the sense of not just passive hearing, but taking what is heard and manifesting the instruction in proper observance. Furthermore, Hebraic thought gives righteous and wicked deeds not just a house but a road/path that we walk on. When on the road to wickedness we "repent", the word *teshuvah* literally means "to turn around" as in getting back on the right road. That is also why Yeshua talked about the road to destruction being broad but the path to life being narrow.

Paul is well aware that Torah itself is not the curse! The curse is the failure to obey Torah! In the letter to the Galatians, Paul then goes on to remind them that one is not *made* righteousness by Torah, but that "the righteous will live by faith". That is, one "lives" by obedience to Torah (Leviticus 18:5), and by the "faith" that Torah is of the Creator and in the Mashiyach's redemption for our crimes (John 17:3). Paul draws this very conclusion as he continues in Galatians 3:13 by again citing again from the Tanach:

Deuteronomy 21:22. If someone has committed a sin that merits a judgment of death and you execute him and hang him on a tree, 23. his corpse shall not hang the entire night on the tree and so therefore you must surely bury him on the exact same day--because a person who has been hanged is cursed by Elohim—so that you will not make unclean your land that YHWH your Elohim is giving you as an inheritance.

However, one must look at the *previous verse* in Deuteronomy 21, to understand exactly what Paul's reference means. Verse 22: *"If someone has committed a sin that merits a judgment of death, and you execute him and hang him on a tree..."* See, we are the ones cursed by our crimes! Not Torah! Mashiyach redeems us for our failure to obey

Torah, but this does not mean we no longer need to obey Torah!

Furthermore, Yeshua was "accursed" by his accusers, but instead Christians teach that YAHWEH and Torah accused Yeshua. Yeshua, however, was the Perfect Lamb. He never broke Torah; and therefore He could never come under any curse of Torah. But we do come under the curse when we sin and refuse to turn to YAHWEH!

Deuteronomy 21:22-23 tells us that if someone committed a capital crime and is put to death and hung on a tree, his body is not to remain on that tree overnight, but be buried that same day – because a person who has been hanged has been cursed by God. Yeshua committed no capital crime. Yet the Pharisees were warning Jews of Yeshua by arguing that he had become a curse because he had hung on the torture stake. They tried everything in their power to vilify Yeshua before the Jewish people. According to Andrew Gabriel Roth:

Paul [in his letter to the Galatians] is repeating this accusation of the Pharisees for the benefit of "Messianic Pharisees" (Galatians 2:4) who were likely weary of being shunned by their people (see Matthew 10:39) and wanted back into the synagogues; and so they were posturing themselves as Ebionites. "Messianic Pharisees" or Ebionites, attend Orthodox synagogues and are enamored with traditional Rabbinical Judaism; they believe Yeshua is Mashiyach, but not the Arm of YAHWEH or YAHWEH Tsidkenu revealed. Paul is using the strongest words possible to affirm the Truth by reminding certain Galatians that they are trying to dilute the Netzarim Faith with traditional Pharisaism. In 2,000 years little has changed; many Orthodox Rabbis still call Yeshua a bastard and a curse of the Jewish people because he "hung on the stake." Some Rabbis will even provide a mock funeral for Jews who follow Yeshua, and teach that the family member is as though they never existed; so if one can understand the duress that certain "Messianic Pharisees" were under, then one can understand why Paul chose such severity of words.

Continuing with Galatians 3:

Galatians 3:21. Is the Torah we received against the promises of Elohim? Elohim forbid! For if Torah had been given, which was able to give life, then truly righteousness would have come as a result of Torah.

Paul, here, had just described, in verses 14-20, that Torah was *not* the Promise, and that Torah is *not the fulfillment* of the Promise either. But Torah is a very big deal in the Rabbinical Jewish world from which the Apostle Paul came. The point that Paul makes over and over is that while Torah is a very big deal, the giver of Torah is even bigger! YAHWEH gave Torah as a Faith component of Covenant (terms and conditions) between Him and His people, so don't disregard Him or put Him on the shelf simply because you believe yourself to be a Torah scholar. Worse yet, don't put up fences and traditions that become more important than YAHWEH and His Mashiyach. Torah has been given a "bad rap" over the centuries precisely because of these fences and traditions of so-called "Torah experts". Most Christians will go to a pastor or anyone they think smarter than themselves to ask extremely important questions about God and His Messiah, long before they even consider going to YAHWEH Himself! Faith demands a person enter into an active relationship with YAHWEH and His Messiah, regardless as to whether a person is Christian or Jewish.

*Galatians 3:22. But the Scripture has encircled all things and put them under sin, that the promise in the faith of Y'shua the Mashiyach might be given to those who believe. 23. **But before faith came, Torah was guarding us** while we were confined from the faith* *about to be revealed. 24. Torah was therefore a tutor for us, going towards the Mashiyach that we, by faith, might be made righteous. 25. But since faith came, we are no longer under tutors. 26. For you are all the children of Elohim by faith in Y'shua the Mashiyach.*

Is Paul nullifying Torah by saying "Torah was guarding us before faith came"? Certainly not! Remember, the faith aspect of this relationship is that you *believe* the Mashiyach came to die for your sins, and by His death, you have the opportunity for everlasting life. But Torah *defines* your righteousness – it was (and is) your tutor, as Paul illustrates.

In this regard "Torah" can be compared with any righteous values a person voluntarily imposes upon himself. However, as a spiritual relationship is established with YAHWEH and Yeshua, a soul is elevated to much higher levels of spiritual awareness and accountability. Therefore, it is a complete farce when Christians claim to follow Mashiyach, but willfully violate Torah according to their denominational authorities. (See Matthew 7:23.)

Many Christians insist there is nothing in the New Covenant that commands us to be Torah observant, or which suggests we continue to adhere to any of the commands of the "Old Testament." But, if that were the case, then how would they explain Romans 3:31?

Romans 3:31. Do, we then nullify Torah by faith? May it never be! On the contrary, we establish Torah.

Please ask yourself while reading the following scripture whether Paul was negating Torah, or in any way suggesting that being kosher, or keeping any of the festivals or the seventh day Sabbath was now taboo....You'll quickly see that he was **not**; he was merely warning about the **opinions of men** concerning these things – He was not giving permission to ignore the rules!

Colossians 2:16. Let no (pagan) therefore judge you about food and drink, or about the distinctions of festivals and new moons and Shabbats 17. which were shadows of the things then future; but the body of Mashiyach.

Most Bible versions translate the above as "let no one therefore judge"; but the AENT puts this back into context to show that the Body of Mashiyach must not be concerned with the judgments of those who are outside the Kingdom of Elohim; that is, those who don't know Torah or Mashiyach. It is clear, given the location of this audience and the fact that the Apostle Paul always references Jews directly, that Paul is addressing the local talk of the pagans whose religion dominated this region.

Compare this with Colossians 1:24. Paul is stating that the "Body of Mashiyach" determines how to observe Torah, including Kashrut (kosher), Shabbats, *Mo'edim* (YAHWEH's Appointed Times/Feasts) and *Rosh Chodeshim* (Biblical New Years); therefore, don't let lawless pagans judge you; they have their own religious customs and way of doing things! For example, many choose to attend "religious" meetings on Sun-Day, and they have sunrise services on Ishtar (Easter), then for December 25th they put up a Tammuz (Christmas) tree that commemorates the rebirth of the Babylonian deity Tammuz (god of fertility and of new life). And the gold and silver balls that Christians hang on their Christmas trees originally represented the testicles of Tammuz, as he was renown for "pleasing the ladies."

Most Christians know full well that Yeshua was not born on December 25th, but the pagan celebrations have become such entrenched traditional rituals that truth has become an embarrassing inconvenience. In other words, don't let family, friends, pastors, or co-workers judge you for observing truthful Torah festivals, because their motive is for you to return to the pagan substitutes they themselves prefer.

The Church today is following in the idolatrous footsteps of ancient and modern Israel according to Ezekiel 8:14 and Jeremiah 10 and 17. The vast majority of Christians twist these verses to teach that Shabbat and the Feasts of YAHWEH "were fulfilled by Christ and are no longer necessary" which completely contradicts what Paul taught – that YAHWEH's Feasts are a shadow of things to come; not to mention, they are rehearsals for the Bride of Mashiyach! What Mashiyach and Paul call "good," Christianity calls evil; even suggesting their pagan based rituals are sanctified through a "Christian" label (see Isaiah 5:14-23).

Romans 14:5. One man discriminates between days; and another judges all days alike. But let every one be sure in regard to his knowledge. 6. He that esteems a day, esteems (it) for his Master: and he that esteems not a day for his Master, he does not esteem (it). And he that eats, eats to his Master and gives thanks to Elohim: and he that eats not to his Master he eats not and gives thanks to Elohim.

Does the above suggest that Paul said it is up to each of us to decide what we should eat and what day we should keep?

Absolutely not! The context of this passage was a dispute over whether one can eat food that may or may not have been offered to idols. In those days food that may or may not have been offered to idols was usually put out for sale to people on a certain day of the week – and some believers refused to purchase or eat food on those days, just to be on the safe side. On the other hand, some did because they figured, since they didn't know for sure whether or not it had been offered, it wouldn't be wrong to eat it.

In the previous Scripture (Romans 14:5-6) Paul was not addressing kosher foods or Sabbath day observance at all; he was referring to the disagreement over whether market place food, because of idolatry, should be bought and eaten on a certain day of the week.

Please check out David H. Stern's explanation in the preface of his Complete Jewish Bible, wherein he demonstrates the difference between "kosher" and "ceremonially clean." Stern says YAHWEH **never** said pork, shellfish, etc. were food. People called these animals food in rebellion against God....

The passages in Romans are dealing with animals YAHWEH gave us to eat and whether they are ceremonially clean and can be eaten at that time. Even in Peter's vision (Acts 11), Peter would never have eaten the kosher animals that had been in contact with *treif* (non-kosher) animals. The vision was to show that, as Peter knew which animals were clean and which were not because as God had shown him, Peter was to accept the Gentiles as God had now shown him they were "clean". The rest of the passage in Acts 11 shows that this is the correct interpretation and what the vision was all about (see Acts 11:18).

Now, consider the following passage from the book of Hebrews which many Christians attempt to use to show that the Old Covenant of Moses (which was all about Torah!) was completely replaced:

Hebrews 10:8. He first said: Sacrifices and oblations and holocausts for sins which were offered according to Torah, you did not desire; 9. and afterwards he said: Behold I come to do your will, O Elohim: hereby, he abolished the former that he might establish the latter.

Does the above recommend **abolition** of the Mosaic Covenant? No! Since we know that YAHWEH and not Moses was the author of Torah, and that Torah dates all the way back to Adam and Eve, when read in context, we can see that through Yeshua the covenant wasn't abolished but merely transformed/revised/clarified/updated to meet God's needs for the sake of the next generation of Earth's population explosion!

Hebrews 2:17 explains what Hebrews 10:8-9 is all about:

Hebrews 2:17. And so it was right that he should be in all respects like his Brothers; that he might be merciful and a high priest faithful in the things of Elohim, and might make expiation for the sins of the people. 18. For, in that he himself has suffered and been tempted, he is able to succor them who are tempted.

YAHWEH no longer required sin sacrifices, thanks to the New Covenant Sin sacrifice of Yeshua. In Hebrews 2:17 Paul attempts to explain that the animal sin sacrifice does not take away sins, but that Yeshua's sacrifice renders useless any other offering for sin. Then, in Hebrews 5:13-6:1 He relates the importance of the Messiah to the maturing of intellect.

Nowhere in Hebrews or anywhere else, for that matter, does Paul ever claim that Torah has been abolished! On the contrary, he explains that those who disobey Torah remain guilty, and that if they ignore the shed blood of Yeshua they will face severe judgment. Furthermore, Paul, throughout Hebrews 10, refers to being "made holy"– explaining that holiness isn't obtained just by believing in Messiah but by observing Torah (see Numbers 15:40 and Proverbs 4:2).

Now, let's examine Ephesians 2:15-16 to see whether it implies that Yeshua abolished Torah:

Ephesians 2:15. And in his flesh (the) enmity and regulations of commands (contained) in his commandments are abolished (so) that in himself (an occurrence of the divine nature, or qnoma), he might make the two into one, establishing peace.

Qnoma can mean "core substance" or "occurrence." Although Greek reads "self" Aramaic does not; "self" leads to assumptions of "personhood" which breeds idolatry.

The grammatical structure of Ephesians 2:15 reveals that the "customs" (traditions of the Pharisees) were abolished; not Torah. Mashiyach abolishes the "enmity" (hatred or animosity) that has been brought against YAHWEH by religious tradition and false interpretations of Torah, which was a heavy burden that people could not bear. Christian theologians, however, twist this verse and teach that it was YAHWEH's Torah that brought the hatred and that Mashiyach did away with Torah, which is a very reckless and evil theology. Mashiyach sent the *Ruach haKodesh* (Holy Spirit) to write YAHWEH's Torah upon the hearts of his people, not abolish it.

Consequently, there's nothing to imply that Torah was negated. When Yeshua was physically present on Earth, He attempted to show how senseless was the animosity between the two groups caused by the opinions of men concerning Torah. Through Him, "one new man" was made from the two separate groups.

Colossians 2:20. For if you are dead with the Mashiyach from the rudiments of the world, why are you judged as if you were living in the world? 21. But, you do not touch and you do not taste and you do not handle: 22. for these things perish in the using; and they are the commandments and doctrines of men.

In the above, did Paul say we are to ignore the Old Testament commandments today? No – absolutely not! He's again talking about the opinions of men, not about YAHWEH's Word which has always been holy and good!

In Colossians 2:23, Paul attempted to thwart the creation of more human opinions by writing:

23. And they seem to have a kind of wisdom in a show of humility and of the Fear of Elohim, and of not sparing the body; not in anything of excellence, but in things subservient to the body.

Many Christians argue that Paul said we could eat whatever we want, meaning there is no more *kashrut/kosher* (the set of dietary laws governing what can or cannot be eaten). Please read the following passage very carefully:

1 Timothy 4:1. But the Spirit says explicitly that, in the latter times, some will depart from the faith, and will go after deceptive spirits and after the doctrine of demons. 2. These will seduce by a false appearance, and will speak a lie and will be seared in their conscience; 3. and will forbid to marry, and will require abstinence from meats which Elohim has created for use and for thankfulness by them who believe and know the truth. 4. Because whatever is created by Elohim is good; and there is nothing which should be rejected if it be received with thankfulness, 5. for it is sanctified by the Word of Elohim and by prayer.

"Forbid to marry" in the context of 1 Timothy 4 refers to the Roman Catholic church and other Christian organizations forbid priests to marry; by installing their own so called "infallible" deity-like "fathers" they've chosen to wage war against Torah and Mashiyach Yeshua. See also Matthew 23:9.

Christians have interpreted verse 4 as all foods being declared "good". This is quite wrong! First, we have to remember that Paul was talking to the Jews who ate only kosher foods. They wouldn't dream of going against what YAHWEH said in Leviticus about what He considered to be food. Kosher Law is still God's Law, and Paul actually confirmed that fact. In 1 Timothy 4, he warned against "doctrines of demons" which say one can't have certain foods which God has said are good to eat. Paul is saying every clean creature is good and not to be refused **if** it is made holy by the Word of God and prayer (thanksgiving).

It is understood which foods are "clean" and which are not. Leviticus tells us what is holy and not holy. The word kosher comes from the same root as *kodesh*, meaning holy.

Food includes meat which must be sanctified by the Word of Elohim (Torah), and there are clean and unclean meats – some are sanctified, some are not; see Leviticus 11. Saying a prayer over unclean food doesn't sanctify the food anymore than praying that you don't get caught stealing can "sanctify" or protect you from the consequences of that transgression. Many fail to remember that, just because the punishment is not immediate, doesn't mean that it's been forgotten by heaven.

The books of Leviticus and Deuteronomy specify what can and cannot be consumed. According to YAHWEH's Torah, the animals considered "clean" have cloven hooves and ruminate (chew their cud). Swine are considered to be unclean because, while their hooves are cloven, they don't chew their cud. Paul knew this; he did not negate or change it. (And if he **had ever** attempted to show that any part of Torah had been negated or abolished, we would have to ask ourselves: Who are we to believe – the **Divine Yeshua**, the Word of YAHWEH in the flesh, who was completely Torah observant, or the **human**, Paul? If Paul had truly been anti-Torah as the Church suggests, then surely YAHWEH wouldn't have allowed the writings of Paul to be included in the Bible!)

Although it may not make sense to our limited human mindsets, YAHWEH had His reasons for *kashrut* laws, and if you don't have access to a computer, it would behoove you to buy a good book on this subject because it's extremely important.

Getting back to YAHWEH's Torah:

It cannot be overemphasized that Yeshua abolished the need for sin sacrifices and that He came to abolish the "rabbinical" teachings of the time that had people so bound up in "legalism" that they were afraid to get out of bed on the Sabbath for fear of being guilty of "working." The teachings of the rabbis of old had made the entire Torah a burden:

Acts 21:20. And when they heard (it) they glorified Elohim. And they said to him: "Our brother, You see how many myriads there are in Judaea who have believed: and these are all zealous for Torah! 21. And it has been told them, of you, that you teach all the Jews that are among the Gentiles to depart from Moshe, by telling them not to circumcise their children, and not to observe the rites of Torah. 22. Now, because they have heard that you have arrived here, 23. do what we tell you. We have four men, who have vowed to purify themselves. 24. Take them, and go and purify yourself with them, and pay the expenses along with them, as they will shave their heads; that every one may know, that what is said against you is false, and that you fulfill and observe Torah. 25. As to those of the Gentiles who have believed, we have written, that they should keep themselves from (an idol's) sacrifice, and from sexual sin, and from what is strangled, and from blood." 26. Then Paul took those men, on the following day, and was purified with them; and he entered and went into the temple, explaining to them how to complete the days of the purification, up to the presentation of the offering by each of them.

Let's ask ourselves this: If Yeshua had indeed abolished the "law," then why did the apostle Paul observe it with four other church men in Yerushalayim (Jerusalem) 29 years **after** the crucifixion of Messiah (Acts 21:23-24)?

This event clearly establishes the Apostle Paul as a Torah observant Jew. However, mainstream Christianity twists Paul into being a man pleaser – as though his offering was solely to please Jews, as some sort of political posturing.

There is no conflict between atonement made by Yeshua's blood and the giving of offerings in the Temple. Paul walks in the footsteps of Yeshua, King David, and all the Yisrael of Elohim, when he declares *"I rejoice in the Torah of Elohim, in the inner man."* (Romans 7:22.) Each and every blood sacrifice and offering made in the Temple points to Mashiyach's perfect blood. The Temple stood until 70 CE and the followers of Yeshua met there to give offerings unto YAHWEH, but they also knew atonement was accomplished through the precious blood of Yeshua!

Attacks against Paul by factions of rabbinical zealots were manifold. Paul taught that faith and intent of the heart determines whether a person is ready to be circumcised and walk in Torah. At no time did he teach against either circumcision or Torah; however, he opposed the "traditions of the Pharisees" who demanded blind observance to their religious traditions. Paul required that Gentile converts be taught about covenant and have clear understanding of what they were doing, in relationship to YAHWEH and His Mashiyach. Both the Pharisees and Netzarim taught that a person must study to develop their understanding and establish the intent in their heart before circumcision, rather than blindly follow the wishes of others. Only a small group of zealots demanded immediate circumcision, which is something Paul clearly opposes. It is very evident that Abraham received instruction before his circumcision, and he is the father of Faith for both Jews and Gentiles alike.

Paul wrote:

Romans 7:7. *What will we say then? Is Torah sin? May it never be!* ***For I had not learned sin except by means of Torah:*** *for I had not known lust, had not Torah said, You will not covet.*

Romans 7:12. *As a result, Torah is* ***Set Apart****; and the Commandment is Set Apart, and righteous, and good. 13. Did that* *which is good, therefore, become death to me? May it never be! But sin, that it might be seen to be sin, perfected death in me by means of that good (Torah); that sin might the more be condemned by means of the Commandment. 14. For we know, that Torah is spiritual; but I am carnal, and sold to sin.*

Paul says "Torah is spiritual"; therefore, while those without Torah might be very religious, they are not "spiritual" according to Paul and Mashiyach! Mashiyach is the goal and we are to be like him, which means that when our spirits are awakened to Mashiyach we will proceed to welcome Torah to be written upon our hearts. Consider this:

2 Corinthians 4:18. While we look not at these seen things, but at those not seen; for these seen things are temporary, but those not seen are eternal.

So, the question once more is: Why would Yeshua's death have abolished Torah? Those who teach contrary to the Torah, which both Yeshua and Paul upheld, are false preachers and prophets; nothing more, nothing less. Paul wrote:

2 Corinthians 11:13. For they are false apostles, crafty workers, and pretend apostles of the Mashiyach. 14. And in this there is nothing strange. For if Satan pretends to be a Messenger of light, 15. it is no great thing if his ministers pretend to be ministers of righteousness whose end will be according to their works.

Again – is Torah still valid today? You bet it is! It is our standard for righteousness. Yeshua said that not one *yud* (smallest letter in the Hebrew alphabet) or tittle (a small distinctive mark such as a diacritic/accent or the dot over an i or a j) would pass away, and that those who love Him will keep His commandments. **Torah is not for salvation**, but for sanctification (being Holy).

Regardless as to how much the Christian world struggles to prove otherwise, the fact is, **Paul taught the Kingdom of Elohim**, testifying of Messiah Yeshua and Torah. As Acts 28:23 clearly shows, Paul taught *"out of the Torah of Moshe, and out of the prophets,"* from morning till evening. He also gave a very stern warning when he said:

Hebrews 10:28. For if he who transgressed the Torah of Moshe, died without mercies at the mouth of two or three witnesses; 29. how much more, do you think, will he receive capital punishment who has trodden upon the Son of Elohim and has accounted the blood of his covenant by which he is sanctified, as the blood of all men and has treated the Spirit of grace in an insulting manner?

By comparing YAHWEH's capital punishment from the Torah of Moshe with violations against the "blood of his covenant" or against the "Spirit of grace" Paul clearly taught that Torah is a Living Covenant that was **never** abolished!

No one can keep the Torah perfectly (but thanks to Yeshua we are forgiven!) However, striving to live as ELOHIM commands brings us closer to His desire for our lives.

Questions for Chapter 5

After reading Chapter 5 (and referring to your Bible), you should be able to answer the following questions. You may then compare your answers with those in the Appendix:

Question 1: What, exactly, was accomplished when Yeshua martyred Himself as our Final SIN Sacrifice?

Question 2: Colossians 2:14 tells us He (Yeshua) wiped away the "bill of charges" or "our debts" against us. Romans 3:31 says: *Do, we then nullify Torah by faith? May it never be! On the contrary, we establish Torah.* Cite here any scriptures in the Gospels where man was ever told that Torah was abolished.

Question 3: Please explain in your own words what the following passage means: Romans 2:*12. For those without Torah, who sin, will also perish without Torah; and those under the Torah, who sin, will be judged by the Torah. 13. **For not the hearers of the Torah are righteous before Elohim; but the doers of the Torah** are being made righteous. 14. For if Gentiles who have not the Torah shall, by their nature, do the things of the Torah; they, while without the Torah, become a Torah to themselves. 15. Additionally, they show the work of the Torah as it is inscribed on their hearts; and their conscience bears testimony to them, their own reflections rebuking or vindicating one another. 16. (And that vindication is for) in the day in which Elohim will judge the secret [actions] of men, as my tidings [teaches], by Y'shua the Mashiyach.*

Question 4: Romans 14 says: *5. One man discriminates between days; and another judges all days alike. But let every one be sure in regard to his knowledge. 6. He that esteems a day, esteems (it) for his Master: and he that esteems not a day for his Master, he does not esteem (it). And he that eats, eats to his Master and gives thanks to Elohim: and he that eats not to his Master he eats not and gives thanks to Elohim.* Where or how does this passage suggest that Paul said it is up to each of us to decide what we should eat and what day we should keep?

Question 5: The books of Leviticus and Deuteronomy specify what can and cannot be consumed. Although it may not make sense to most of us, the bottom line is, YAHWEH doesn't want us to consume "garbage disposals" – those animals specifically designed to clean up the bottoms of rivers and oceans and streets and forests by eating other dead animals, etc. Can you name some of those "garbage disposals" and describe why we should adhere to the command today to NOT eat them?

Question 6: Torah is not for salvation, but for _____.

Question 7: As Acts 28:23 clearly shows, Paul taught from _____.

Question 8: In your own words, please explain what Peter's vision meant in Acts 11.

Question 9: Cite the scripture where Rav Sha'ul (Apostle Paul) suggests that, since Yeshua's death, we can eat whatever we want, meaning there is no more "Kosher"?

Question 10: How did the death of Yeshua create the idea that "unclean" animals are now considered "clean"?

Question 11: Was Yeshua Torah observant? Were His disciples and the Apostles? How do you know?

Question 12: Apostle Paul was caught being Torah observant 29 years AFTER Messiah's death (Acts 21:23-24). And Paul said: *"What will we say then? Is Torah sin? May it never be! For I had not learned sin except by means of Torah: for I had not known lust, had not Torah said, You will not covet"....* (Romans 7:7). He also said: *"Torah is Set Apart; and the Commandment is Set Apart, and righteous, and good."* (Romans 7: 12) What then, would make someone believe he spoke against the Torah and suggested Christians don't have to bother with it?

Question 13: If you had to pick one or the other to follow, whose teachings would you pick – Yeshua's or Paul's? Why?

Question 14: What is meant by "Unless your righteousness **surpasses** those of the Pharisees and the teachers of the Torah you shall surely not enter into the kingdom of heaven" (Matthew 6:20)? How was righteousness established **at that time** if not by Torah?

Question 15: Yeshua said in Matthew 19:17, *"Now if you desire to enter into life, keep the Commandments."* If Christians are "free from the law" as they say, then why does Yeshua *explain* from the commandments of the "Old Testament"? For instance:

*Matthew 5:38. You **have heard that it has been said** that an eye for an eye and a tooth for a tooth. 39. **But I say to you** that you should not stand against evil, but who hits you upon your right cheek, turn also to him the other.*

"You have heard it said" refers to oral tradition and/or man's interpretation of what was written in Torah. But when Yeshua says "I say to you" or "it is written" He is *explaining* the proper meaning of those laws. So, what, exactly, are Christians free from?

Question 16: According to the Gospels, the Apostles were not learned scholars. We are told they were fishermen, a tax collector, a tent maker – "blue collar" types. In those days, they had to go through a great ordeal to document their experiences with Yeshua, which included gaining access to Papyrus on which to write down their accounts. As far as we know the only Apostle who could speak a foreign language was Paul, who spoke some Greek. In view of this, do you really believe the Apostles would have written the Gospels in Greek? Why or why not?

Chapter 6

What parts of Torah can we still observe today?

Notes:

If we're talking about all of YAHWEH's various commands and "do's" and "don'ts" in general, the logical answer is: We need to observe whatever we possibly can, to the best of our abilities.

Many people believe Torah consists only of "those old 613 commandments." The truth is, while YAHWEH did hand down the Commandments, He never numbered them. The idea originated in the Talmud ("Oral Torah" which consists of the ideas of the ancient rabbis who were desperately trying to understand the Word of YAHWEH) which says there are both "positive" and "negative" *mitzvot* (do's and don'ts) which can be divided into 365 Negative *Mitzvot* (which we are told remind us every day of the year to keep us from doing bad things) plus 248 Positive *Mitzvot* (coincidentally the number of bones in the human body) for a total of 613.

Correspondingly, the *tzitzit* (knotted fringes) of the *tallit* (prayer shawl which "the people of Israel" are to wear - Numbers 15:38 and Deuteronomy 22:12) are also connected to the 613 commandments. Torah commentator Rashi suggested that the number of knots on a *tzitzit* (in its Mishnaic spelling) has the value of 600. When doubled over, each tassel has eight threads and five sets of knots, totaling 13 - for a grand total of 613. Thus, wearers of a *tallit* are reminded of all Torah commandments.

Alternatively, since each letter of the Hebrew alphabet has a numerical value, one can also tie the knots of *tzitzit* in a way that causes them to spell out the Name of YAHWEH. When Yeshua returns atop a white horse as "King of Kings, and Master of Masters written upon His thigh," (Rev. 19:11-13,16) the *tzitzits* of His *tallit* will fall - where else, but across his thighs....

Moving on, of the "613 Commandments" most cannot be kept today because they were prescribed for the priests and kings of the day, while some were only for men and others for women. However, there were some commandments that were meant to last **forever**. These include:

- **The Ten Commandments:** (Please see Exodus 20; 31:18; 34:29; Deuteronomy 5:5 which included several "forever" commandments).

- **The Seventh Day Sabbath:** (Genesis 2:3; Exodus 20:8; 31:13; 31:16-17; Leviticus 23:3; Deuteronomy 5:12; Isaiah 66:23 and Isaiah 58:13).

- **The Biblical feasts:** Outlined in Leviticus 23 which states after each feast: *"it shall be a statute for ever in all your dwellings throughout your generations."*

- **Keeping kosher.** Yes, eating "clean" foods was a "forever" command. For a complete outline, see Deuteronomy 14:1-21 and Leviticus 11.

The above is by no means exhaustive, but can be counted among some of the most visible of the *mitzvot*.

Man has always liked to "pick and choose" when it comes to the Bible, but it's time to learn some of those "forever" commands – including the concept of the seventh-day Sabbath and the Biblical feasts which are YAHWEH's appointed times. Each one is significant in that Yeshua is foreshadowed in them. As a matter of fact, Yeshua has so far only "fulfilled" the first four of the seven feasts – and the next one should be what Christians are calling the "Rapture." Let's discuss these a little further....

Why should we keep the Biblical feasts?

The original and eternal Feasts of YAHWEH are everlasting appointments between YAHWEH and His People and are clearly prophesied to carry on into the Seventh Millennium and beyond into the world to come.

Isaiah 66:23 From New Moon (month) to New Moon and from Shabbat to Shabbat, all humanity will come and bow down before Me, says YHWH.

YAHWEH designed His appointed times, the *mo'edim*, for His people to come together to worship Him. The fact that all flesh will one day worship YAHWEH according to **one** calendar tells us that the *mo'edim* are not for Jews only, but for all the Household of Faith as One Body. ("His people" includes anyone who has been "grafted in" to the Olive Tree [Isra'el] to worship the risen Messiah.)

The Creator appointed seven feasts to be celebrated each year:

- Passover (Pesach)

- Unleavened Bread (Hag HaMatzot)

- Firstfruits (Yom HaBikkurim)

- Fifty days after Firstfruits is the Feast of Weeks (Shavuot)

- Feast of Trumpets (Rosh Hashanah)

- Day of Atonement (Yom Kippur)

- Feast of Tabernacles (Sukkot)

YAHWEH, who is continuously revealing Himself to us, provided some interesting clues to show the importance of His appointed times! The first three major events for believers in Yeshua (His death, burial and resurrection) happened on the first three feasts, and the presentation of the Holy Spirit (what Christians refer to as Pentecost) came 50 days later:

- While Passover was being celebrated (which included the slaying of an unblemished lamb) our Savior, was being slain on the stake (1 Corinthians 5:7).

- The Feast of Unleavened Bread is a foreshadowing of sanctification as Yeshua was buried. Leaven represents sin and, as you know, Yeshua was sinless.

- Firstfruits, celebrated on the morning after the first Sabbath following the feast of Unleavened Bread (Leviticus 23:10-11), is symbolic of Yeshua being the Firstfruits (1 Corinthians 15:23).

- Shavuot (the Feast of Weeks) celebrates the first-fruits of the wheat harvest and the giving of the Torah. It also commemorates the giving of the Holy Spirit to the gathering of believers in Jerusalem (Acts 2), and it fell on the next feast 50 days later (on what Christians call Pentecost)!

Since Yeshua has fulfilled the first four feasts, we can probably assume that the next big event - the so-called "Rapture" - could fall on the next scheduled feast day, Rosh Hashanah ("Jewish Civil New Year"/Feast of Trumpets), when YAHWEH calls his people together (Leviticus 23:23-25). It is the start of the civil year in the Hebrew calendar which was instituted by YAHWEH Himself in Exodus 12:2. Rosh

Hashanah is observed as a day of rest and is characterized by the blowing of the shofar (a trumpet made from a ram's horn), intended to awaken the listener from his or her "slumber" and alert them to the coming judgment.

There is, of course, much more to YAHWEH's feasts, but the bottom line is: Judging from the importance that HE placed on them, why would anyone think "Jesus abolished" them?

Some have questioned as to how Yeshua could fulfill any feasts after His death. The answer is simple: Because God is forever; He has no beginning and no end. The fleshly body He sent temporarily to teach us about Himself died, but His Spirit didn't. We know He is alive because He rose and because no body was ever found in the sealed tomb in which He was buried! The Bible tells us that Yeshua was with His Father YAHWEH at the beginning (John 1:1-2) and that He remains a priest forever (Hebrews 7:3).

YAHWEH's timeline

Man tends to view things from a linear viewpoint and timeline, whereas YAHWEH does not. He's God, so why should He have to fulfill everything within our concept of time? His feasts were given for a reason – in part, so that man could know what all was supposed to happen and what was yet to come; that is also why Yeshua is foreshadowed in each one of them!

Since God is the same yesterday, today and forever (Hebrews 13:8), why would He suddenly want us to ignore His feasts/appointed times? Does it make sense that, just because Yeshua died, it would automatically negate the other three feasts He has yet to fulfill?

Proverbs 3:1. *"My son, do not forget my teaching [Torah], but keep my commands in your heart."*

Proverbs 6:23. For the mitzvah (Commandment) is a lamp and the Torah-instruction is the light and the way to Life is the strong rebuke that disciplines.

Psalms 1:1. Happy are those who have turned aside from the counsel of the wicked and don't stand with the same path as the sinners or sit where the scornful congregate. 2. But their delight is in the Torah-instruction of YHWH and on His [whole] Torah they meditate on day and night. 3. They are like trees firmly planted by streams of water which yield their fruit in their proper season and whose leaves do not wither away. And they are successful in all that they do.

Deuteronomy 6:4. Shema Yisrael! YHWH Elohaynu, YHWH echad! Hear O'Israel! YHWH is your Elohim; YHWH is One. 5. And you shall love YHWH your Elohim with all your innermost being and with all your life-passion and with all the force you can muster. 6. And these Words, which I am commanding you this very day, are to reside within your innermost being, 7. and you are to teach them with great care to your children. You are to discuss them thoroughly when you sit at home, when you are traveling on the road, when you lie down and when you rise up. 8. You will bind them on your hand as a sign, and put them in the front of your forehead attached to a headband wrapped around it. 9. Then you are to write them upon the door frames of your house and upon your gates.

Before we go on, did you notice verse 4 which said, "…Hear, Isra'el…"? Who is Isra'el again?

Let's discuss the seventh-day Sabbath….

Keeping the Sabbath, one of the Ten Commandments, was not a suggestion! The Bible promises spiritual blessings for those who keep the Sabbath on the day YAHWEH set apart as holy.

Isaiah 56:1. Thus says YHWH: Preserve justice, and do righteousness, for My Salvation is close and approaching, and My righteousness is about to be revealed. 2. Happy is the man who does this and whose son clings fast to it; who keeps himself from polluting the Shabbat and prevent his hand from any evil act.

*Isaiah 56:4. For YHWH has said: As for the eunuchs who preserve my Shabbats and choose to do what delights Me and clings tenaciously to My covenant, to them I will give, 5. in My house and within My walls, a monument and a name superior to that of sons and daughters. I will give them an eternal name which will never be cut off. 6. **And the foreigners who join themselves to YHWH**, to serve Him and to love the Name of YHWH, and to be His servants, **all who guard the Shabbat and do not pollute it**, and cling tenaciously to My covenant, 7. I will bring them to My Set-Apart mountain and make them joyful in My house of prayer.*

YAHWEH blessed the seventh day and even observed it, Himself (Genesis 2:2-3). The Word tells us the seventh day of the week is God's holy Sabbath day for as long as heaven and earth shall last (Exodus 20:8-11, Matthew 5:17-19, 1 John 3:4).

Isaiah 58:13. If you turn your foot back from pursuing your own pleasures because of the Shabbat and call the Shabbat a delight and the Set-Apart day of YHWH honorable and then show honor by not going to your own paths or striking bargains, 14. then you can look for the delight of YHWH, and I will set you to ride on the heights of the earth and I will sustain you with the inheritance of your ancestor Ya'akov, for the mouth of YHWH has spoken!

Please note that the Prophets strongly condemned Sabbath desecration (Ezekiel 20:19-24; Ezekiel 22:8, 26, 31; and Jeremiah 17:27). Yeshua, Paul and the other disciples also kept the Sabbath holy (Luke 4:16). As a matter of fact, in Matthew 24:20 Yeshua, who was telling His disciples about future events, said: *"And pray that your flight will not be in winter, nor on the Shabbat."* Since YAHWEH commanded the SEVENTH day Sabbath and Yeshua kept the seventh-day Sabbath, He certainly wasn't referring to a SUNDAY Sabbath in the future!

Most are not keeping the true Sabbath!

As mentioned before, both believing Jews and Gentiles regularly attended the synagogue for worship on the seventh day Sabbath (Acts 13:42-44).

The seventh day Sabbath, which the Bible tells us will continue into the new heavens and the new Earth (Exodus 20:12 and 20, Isaiah 66:22-23), is an **eternal covenant and divine Sign** from YAHWEH. It serves as a reminder for us to remember and celebrate His work of creation, sanctification and salvation through His Messiah. Even the "New Testament" gives us the following advice about Sabbath keeping:

Hebrews 4:9. For there remains a Shabbat for the people of Elohim. 10. For he who had entered into his rest has also rested from his works as Elohim did from his. 11. Let us, therefore, strive to enter into that rest; or else we fall short, after the way of those who did not believe. 12. For the Word of Elohim is living and all-efficient and sharper than a two-edged sword, and enters even to the deep penetration of the soul and the spirit, and of the joints and the marrow and the bones, and judges the thoughts and reasonings of the heart: 13. Neither is there any creature which is concealed from before him; but every thing is naked and laid bare before his eyes, to whom we are to give account.

Despite scriptural evidence concerning the Sabbath and its importance, many, if not most Christians will argue to the death that the seventh-day Sabbath was abolished at the cross and changed to Sunday because "Jesus rose on a Sunday." The questions remain, however:

- Did Yeshua really rise on a Sunday?

- And even if He did, where's the scripture to support that YAHWEH ever said His Sabbath is now supposed to be on the first day (Sunday)?

Let's check and see what the Bible shows us about the Resurrection from a "Hebrew perspective" which becomes clear when we allow Scripture to interpret Scripture – and reveals that Yeshua was resurrected toward the end of the Sabbath; not early on a Sunday morning (the first day):

Matthew 12:39. And he answered and said to them, An evil and adulterous generation seeks a sign, and a sign will not be given to it except the sign of Yonan the prophet. 40. For as Yonan was in the belly of the fish three days and three nights, likewise will the Son of man be in the heart of the earth three days and three nights.

Matthew 16:4. An evil and adulterous generation requests a sign. And a sign will not be given to it except the sign of Yonan the prophet.

What was the "sign of Yonah/Jonah"?

Matthew 12:40. For as Yonan was in the belly of the fish three days and three nights, likewise will the Son of man be in the heart of the earth three days and three nights. 41. The Ninevite men will arise in judgment with this generation and condemn it, because they repented by the preaching of Yonan, and behold that one greater than Yonan is present.

The **sign** for which we are searching is "Three days and three nights" (Luke 24:21) from death/burial to resurrection of our Savior.

Matthew 16:21. And from that time onwards, Y'shua began to make known to his disciples that he must go to Urislim and suffer much from the elders and from the chief priests, and scribes. And he would be killed, and on the third day would rise up.

Matthew 17:23. And they will kill him, and on the third day he will rise....

Matthew 20:19. And they will deliver him to the Gentiles, and they will mock him, and they will beat him, and they will execute him on a stake. And he will rise on the third day.

NOTE: (See also Matthew 27:64; Mark 9:31; Mark 10:34; Luke 9:22; Luke 13:32; Luke 18:33; Luke 24:7; Luke 24:46; Acts 10:40; and 1 Corinthians 15:4.) The upright stake was foreshadowed by to the "pole" which Moshe held up in Numbers 21:8, 9. The brass serpent was put upon the pole and when the people looked upon it they were preserved from the deadly venom of the snake. So it is, that when people are bitten by the "spiritual serpent" of Genesis 3:15, they must look to Mashiyach for healing and deliverance. The pole was replaced by the cross which was formerly the symbol of the Babylonian sun god. Julius Caesar and his heir struck coins with symbols of the cross (solar wheel) to commemorate the sun god. The Roman Emperor Constantine was a sun worshipper who became a famous Christian, advancing pagan Christianity throughout the Roman Empire. His version of "Christianity" included many pagan rituals, including Sun-day, Tammuz (Christmas) and Ishtar (Easter) worship. The Greek "stauros" also denotes an upright stake; the verb stauroo means to drive stakes. The Greek "xulon" denotes a timber or a log or any piece of dead wood. Bullinger's Companion Bible notes: "Our English word 'cross' is the translation of the Latin crux; but the Greek stauros no more means a crux than the word 'stick' means a 'crutch.'" (AENT)

A thorough study of the Bible reveals that Yeshua was in the grave three days and three nights, and it tells us that He died on Passover, 14 Nisan, which was during the High Holy Days (Leviticus 23:5).

He was in the grave just before sunset on Wednesday night, according to Scripture (John 19:31); all day Thursday and Thursday night; all day Friday and Friday night, and all day Saturday (as Jonah was in the whale three days and three nights) until just before sunset on Saturday when He was resurrected.

To discern exactly when our Savior rose, it is important to recognize a few things – beginning with the fact that the dawning of a new day according to YAHWEH and the Hebrew calendar is at twilight as it is getting dark; not at first light in the morning:

Genesis 1:5 And Elohim called the light Day, and the darkness He called Night. And there was evening and there was morning the first day.

We also need to note the time that Yeshua was placed into the grave, which was just before sunset – or approximately 5 p.m. (March-April timeframe).

Three days and three nights....

No matter what the days are called on our modern calendars, there is no way that three days and three nights beginning sometime in Wednesday evening can end early on Sunday morning – which is what most Christian scholars are trying to insist.

The Bible tells us that Yeshua died at 3 p.m. (the ninth hour - John 19:14 – the day had only 12 "hours" in this era); that He was buried later that day (John 19:31); and that He was in the grave "three days and three nights."

Matthew 27:46. And about the ninth hour, Y'shua cried out with a loud voice and said, My El! My El! Why have you spared me? (See also Mark 15:33-34 and Luke 23:44)

NOTE: A footnote from the AENT regarding the words "Why have you spared me?" instead of the more common "Why have you forsaken me?" says:

"Y'shua was not necessarily quoting Psalm 22, although the imagery of the Psalm is certainly intended by Matthew. Greek is transliterated Eli, *Eli lama sabacthani,* but Peshitta and Psalm 22 read: *Eli, Eli lama azbatani.*

Many Bibles read "forsaken" from which came a false teaching that the Father left Y'shua destitute (Marcionite thinking). Isaiah 53:4 indicates that "we" reckoned him smitten of Elohim, but it is not YAHWEH who tortured his own son; it was men motivated by religious tradition. Psalm 22 references those who scorned Y'shua for his Faith in YAHWEH, and called him a worm (detested), but Father YAHWEH does not forsake the righteous, nor does He at any time "forsake" His own Son, see Psalm 9:9, 10; 37:25; 71:11; Isaiah 49:14-16.

Y'shua says "Eli" (my El). He is in great physical pain after being brutally tortured; those around him were confused to what he was saying, "Eli-yah" or "Eliyahu". If Hebrew eyewitnesses were not sure of what he was saying, it shouldn't be a surprise that Greek transliteration was also wrong, putting *lama sabacthani* rather than *lemana shabakthani*. Perhaps the reason Y'shua says "why are you sparing me" is because he has proven his commitment by laying down his life and has already endured about 6 hours of the execution! So, it's not a matter of being "forsaken" but that he literally means, "Father, I'm ready, why can't we finish this?" In a matter of moments from saying this, he dies, which fully supports this interpretation." (AENT)

This being just before the High Holy Day (a "High Sabbath," Nissan 15, not a regular Saturday Sabbath), the Judeans wanted Him off the cross and in the grave before sundown so as not to desecrate the holiday, which meant He was in the grave at approximately 5 p.m. by modern time keeping shortly after His crucifixion - which means that three days and three nights later would also fall at approximately 5 p.m. Here are the Scriptures to verify these facts:

John 19:14. And it was the eve of the Paskha (Passover) and it was about the sixth hour, and he said to the Yehudeans, "Behold your King!"

John 19:31. And the Yehudeans, because it was the eve, said, "These bodies should not remain on their stakes because the Shabbat is dawning." For it was a high day, the day of the Shabbat, that they entreated from Peelatos that they might break the legs of those who were nailed to the stake and take them down.

NOTE: *"Shabbat is dawning"* literally refers to the evening before Shabbat; that is, late afternoon. "Dawning" is a metaphor for "the Shabbat beginning/approaching"; confirmed in John 19:42.

Now, many people think this Shabbat fell on a Friday (since God's seven-day cycle begins at sundown on Friday evening). However, as we mentioned above, John 19:14 tells us this "preparation day" was not for a regular Shabbat, but for a High Holy Shabbat. Therefore, the Judeans wanted the bodies of Yeshua and the thieves off the crosses before sundown on Preparation Day, as the next day, Thursday, was a Sabbath.

This means that Yeshua was placed in his grave before sunset that evening, Wednesday.

John 19:41. Now there was a garden in that place that Y'shua was executed in, And in that garden a new tomb that a man had not yet been laid in it. 42. And they placed Y'shua there because the Shabbat was beginning and because the tomb was near.

The above Scripture shows that Yeshua was placed in the heart of the earth approximately 5:00 p.m., or before sunset on the day He died. Three days and three nights must end at the time we start the counting – about 5:00 p.m., or before sunset, that night.

Even on the eve of His death, Yeshua kept and fulfilled the Passover: He died on Wednesday the 14th of Nisan, and He rose some time after 3:00 p.m. on the Sabbath exactly three days later, depending on when He was placed in the grave.

The Sabbath is in commemoration of YAHWEH's rest at Creation (Genesis 2:2), and Yeshua's rest after His redemption of mankind. The Sabbath is for a reminder of the **sign** (three days and three nights) of who Yeshua haMashiyach (Messiah) is: He the Lord of the Sabbath.

Now, exactly how do we know that He died on the 14th of Nisan and that particular 14th of Nisan fell on a Wednesday? Because the 14th of Nisan is the day on which YAHWEH declared that the Feast of Passover should be celebrated **forever** (Leviticus 23; Exodus 12:14)! And because of a series of events that took place just prior to the crucifixion:

- Yeshua, the Passover Lamb, fulfilled Zechariah 9:9 when, on 10 Nisan (a Sabbath - Saturday), He rode into Jerusalem on a donkey, as the people waved palm branches: *Rejoice greatly O daughter of Zion! Raise a triumphal shout O daughter of Jerusalem! Behold your king is coming to you. He is righteous, delivering deliverance (salvation), humbled and riding on a donkey, even on a colt, the foal of a donkey*. The Bible tells us that it was a Sabbath Day's journey from Bethany. He then taught in the Temple for three days: Sunday, Monday and Tuesday. Andrew Roth states that the word "deliverance" here is a double exploitation of the root *yasha* which as a verb means "to deliver" and as a noun "salvation". It is also the root of Yeshua's name (Matthew 1:21).

- As promised in Exodus 12:25-28 there was to be an explanation of the Passover service. This Messianic fulfillment took place when Yeshua showed His disciples how to celebrate the Passover Seder the evening before His death. During this time He explained how **He is** the fulfillment of the Passover seder (Luke 22:14-20 and 1 Corinthians 11:23-26). Just as He delivered the Israelites with a mighty hand from the bondage of Egypt, so He delivered us from the bondage of sin! It was here that He explained the meaning of His person in the Passover elements. Afterwards, He and His disciples went to Gethsemane, where they spent part of the night.

- During the night Yeshua was arrested and we are told that His trial continued until approximately 9 a.m., when He was crucified. At 3:00 p.m. (the 9th hour) on Wednesday He died.

But, how do we know He was resurrected before the weekly Sabbath (what we call "Saturday") ended?

Because Yeshua was buried just before sunset on Wednesday, 14 Nisan. Scripture verifies this. This made that evening, after sunset, the first "night." Then at sunrise Thursday, we have the first "day." The second "night" then, was Thursday night, followed by the second "day," Friday morning; the third night Friday evening, and the third "day" Saturday after sunrise. Thus, Yeshua rose during the daylight hours on the Shabbat, upon completing "3 days and 3 nights." Had He not risen till Shabbat was over, after sunset, he would have been in the grave "3 days and 4 nights." Yeshua rose sometime during the Shabbat, when Mary Magdalene and the other Mary were in observance of the Shabbat (Luke 23:56).

Matthew 28:1. Now in the closing (evening) of the Sabbath, as the first of the week was dawning, came Maryam of Magdala and the other Maryam that they might see the grave.

Andrew Gabriel Roth writes:

Aramaic literally reads *"b'ramsha din b'shabata"*, or "in the evening of the Shabbat". The literal meaning of *ramsha* is "evening" or *erev*, but here it is used idiomatically. The dawn and set of the sun is not the only use; there is the "dawn of a new era" or as John 19:31 reads *"mitil d'shabata negha"*, "the Shabbat was dawning." When we compare other verses that record this event, the time of the day being referred to is clearly more than half a day before literal dawn. In John chapter 19, when they put Y'shua into the tomb, they still refer to it as being "day", both in Aramaic and Greek. The "dawn" metaphor "to begin" is confirmed in John 19:42. A more literal form, *"mitil d'shabata aiala"*, would be read as "the Sabbath was beginning/entering/coming about". What is true for "dawning" is also true of "setting" in the sense of "conclusion", as is meant here. This agrees with Greek version, Aramaic information in Matthew, and with other writers in the NT.

The bottom line is that, by the time the two Marys arrived at Yeshua's tomb, Yeshua was nowhere to be found because He was already gone! Since He died at the ninth hour [3 p.m.], three days and three nights later would make it 3 p.m. on Saturday….

As shown above, the Scriptures – read in context – are abundantly clear as to when our Savior died, when He was buried, and when He was resurrected. He did not rise on Sunday. *Even if He DID, the Bible nowhere tells us that we were allowed to change YAHWEH's seventh day Sabbath to the first day of the week, regardless as to the exact time of His resurrection!* Therefore, there is absolutely no reason for the mainstream Christian church to adhere to the Sunday Sabbath tradition. We can **worship** any day we want, but YAHWEH's **day of rest** has ALWAYS been on the seventh day. That never changed!

The idea of a Sunday sunrise resurrection connects back to Ezekiel 8:16:

Ezekiel 8:16. Then He brought me to the inner court of YHWH's House—and behold!—at the door of the Temple of YHWH, between the porch and the altar, there were about twenty-five men with their backs to the Temple of YHWH and with their faces turned to the east as they worshipped the sun in the east!

Most Christians are turning their backs on Shabbat and Torah and the Word of YAHWEH because they follow a religion that tells them that "Jesus (and/or Paul) did away with the law." But YAHWEH says that He gave Torah so that His people would not turn to these things:

Deuteronomy 4:19. And be careful that you do not lift up your eyes to the sky and behold the sun, moon and stars and everything in the sky, and as a result be led away to bow down and serve them, for YHWH your Elohim has given all of these things to all the peoples under the entire sky.

Christians think it is acceptable to "sanctify" Sunday "in the name of Jesus" and many wouldn't think to bow before the sun and worship it; but nevertheless, they pay homage to institutions that have changed "times and laws" (Daniel 7:25) so whether Christians realize it or not, Sunday worship was ripped right out of paganism and has nothing to do with what Yeshua Himself practiced and taught.

Questions for Chapter 6

After reading Chapter 6 (and referring to your Bible), you should be able to answer the following questions. You may then compare your answers with those in the Appendix:

Question 1: Of the "613 Commandments" most cannot be kept today because they were prescribed for the priests and kings of the day, while some were only for men and others for women. However, there were some commandments that were meant to last "forever" and/or they were to be a "permanent ordinance throughout your generations". Can you name some of them?

Question 2: Since God is the same yesterday, today and forever (Hebrews 13:8), why would He suddenly want us to ignore His feasts/appointed times? Does it make sense that, just because Yeshua died, it would automatically negate the other three feasts He has yet to fulfill? Your thoughts on this?

Question 3: YAHWEH designed His appointed times, the *mo'edim*, for His people to come together to worship Him. The fact that all flesh will one day worship YAHWEH according to one calendar tells us that the *mo'edim* are not for Jews only, but for **all** the Household of Faith as One Body. ("His people" includes anyone who has been "grafted in" to the Olive Tree [Isra'el] to worship the risen Messiah.) Besides the Seventh Day Sabbath which constitutes a "date with God" every Saturday wherein we are to rest from the old week and refresh ourselves for the new, can you name the seven other Feasts which are spread throughout the year and their eternal significance? (Hint: See Leviticus 23.)

Question 4: Even if Yeshua did rise on a Sunday, where's the scripture to support that YAHWEH ever said His Sabbath is now supposed to be on the first day (Sunday)?

Question 5: In 1 Corinthians 5:7-8, what Feast did Paul tell us to observe?

Question 6: The only Bible version in which you will find the word "Easter" is in Acts 12:4 of the King James Version, which basically renders the entire Book of Acts useless since there was no "Easter" before the death of Jesus. What, in your own words does "Easter" have to do with His death and resurrection?

Question 7: After arriving at this point in your workbook and knowing what you now know, please write down exactly what you think was "abolished" or "negated" after the death of Jesus.

Question 8: Please write down a few thoughts about your particular "denomination" and why you belong to the church you attend.

Question 9: What denomination did Jesus adhere to?

Question 10: What was Jesus' assignment on earth? (What did He come to do?)

Question 11:   Describe in your own words what "works" are, and then outline why you believe that keeping the Seventh Day Sabbath and God's seven Feasts would be considered "works."

Question 12:   The following email was written by a female Baptist missionary. Can you detect at least five ways her comments are off the mark?

> "Jesus is His Name, not "Yeshua" which means, "His Name will not be blotted out or obliterated."   And the Word was not printed in Aramaic, it was printed in Greek and for a good reason. Because the True and Living God wanted to make sure that the Pharisees did not change the translation to English and fiddle around with it. Peter, upon this rock I will build my Church, and the gates of hell will not prevail against it!"

Chapter 7

Contrary to popular belief, Acts 15 does not exempt Gentile believers from being Torah observant!

Often, people cite Acts 15 to show that Gentiles are exempt from Torah. But, when read in context, we see an entirely different picture; one which shows that the apostles were seriously discussing which of the commandments should be the first observed by Gentile believers entering the kingdom. Let's examine just a few verses:

Acts 15:19. Because of this (I) say that you should not be those oppressors who from the Gentiles are turning to Elohim. 20. But we will send (word) to them that they should abstain from uncleanness of sacrifices (idols) and from adultery and from things that are strangled and from blood. 21. For from ancient generations in all cities Moshe had preachers in the synagogues that on every Shabbat they read him."

"Idols" in the passage above means: That which is "sacrificed" unto other gods according to YΛHWEH's Word in Deuteronomy 32:17 is sacrificed unto devils. Leviticus 17:12-16 commands that neither Jew nor foreigner consume blood or any animals that die of themselves. As for the word "adultery" Andrew Gabriel Roth suggests: "The prohibition against fornication is wide spectrum, against all manner of physical perversion and spiritual whoredom. These Torah directives are eternally binding on all who follow Yeshua Mashiyach and who seek the *Malchut* (Kingdom) of Elohim."

Roth explains that verse 21 above is a clear fulfillment of Isaiah 56:1-9:

Gentile converts are observing Shabbat and learning Torah as one body along with Jews. Shortly thereafter, Marcion, whom Polycarp referred to as "the firstborn of the devil" built the first all-Gentile church to promote Christo-Paganism. Marcion held his services on Sunday which blended with Zeus (the sun god) culture and projected a hybrid Je-Zeus identity in opposition to the Jewish Mashiyach. The modern theologies of Je-zeus Christos are based more on Hellenism than on original fundamental Hebraic values. Marcion coined the words "Old - New Testament" and did his very best to warn Gentiles away from Torah and "the God of the Old Testament." Marcion invented theologies known as replacement, dispen-sational, supercessionism, etc., which are very popular among Christianity today.

Remember, Gentiles in Paul's day were exposed to Torah on a weekly basis at synagogue, and so Paul surmised that observation of these four rules would ultimately lead to proper obedience of **all** of the Torah. Therefore, the apostles chose the following commandments for Gentiles to begin observing which included abstaining from:

1. things polluted by idols
2. adultery (fornication)
3. animals that had been strangled
4. blood

The following was borrowed and condensed with permission from the Mashiyach.com website.

Abstaining from things polluted by idols:

YAHWEH commanded: *Exodus 20:3.* *"You shall have no other gods before me."*

Eating food that was dedicated to other gods shows allegiance to the people and to the god it was sacrificed to; consequently, it is forbidden.

Anyone who doesn't eat of things "sacrificed to idols" is also being careful to not convert cultural polytheistic values into a Messianic lifestyle. This is not solely about the abstention of certain foods; there are many aspects of community, and status quo values that are attached to things "sacrificed to idols."

The company a person keeps is also being addressed here; this distinction regarding food brings opportunity to introduce others to the Kingdom. This matter of eating things "sacrificed to idols" is so basic and foundational that it has the power to bring souls out of paganism, as do each of the Commandments of YAHWEH. To be a Kedoshim (Set Apart People), is Mashiyach (Messiah), every individual makes a choice to uphold Torah as the Word of YAHWEH, or not.

But false religion presents "alternatives" to the Word of YAHWEH; relativism, removing Set Apart distinctions to make convenient traditions so that people are not embarrassed by truth. Y'shua and his disciples never ate treif, nor things sacrificed to idols; neither would they eat "whatever" was set before them, which is simply a religious projection.

Abstaining from fornication:

Abstinence from fornication means avoiding every form of sexual perversion. However, the broader meaning refers to fornication with cultural deities and lifestyle choices that are rooted in paganism.

The Bride of Mashiyach has a distinct calling to be separate from paganism. The value of each soul is welcome into the Kingdom of Elohim as equals and elevated with the understanding that each one is made in "the image of Elohim." Each is called to put away "the old man," the modern evolutionary gospel that elevates man's achievements, science and religions above the Word of YAHWEH.

Unfortunately, there are many examples within Christianity that cater to the pagan element. For instance, Sunday church services originated with sacrifices to the sun. Easter (Ishtar) was originally a pagan festival that commemorates a sex goddess. "Easter eggs" originated in pagan fertility rituals. "Christmas trees" have their origin with Tammuz (the Branch), a sex god whose admirers put balls on small evergreen trees as testicular remembrances of their male sex god. The small evergreen tree denotes the rebirth of Tammuz.

Abstaining from fornication demands that one not practice the ways of the heathen through fornicating with their deities, or permitting syncretism to bring paganism into "the gospel".

2 Timothy 4:3. For the time will come when they will not give ear to sound teaching; but, according to their lusts, will multiply to themselves teachers in the itching of their hearing; 4. and will turn away their ears from the truth, and incline after fables. 5. But be vigilant in all things; and endure evils and do the work of a proclaimer of the Good News, and fulfill your ministry.

Abstaining from food that was strangled:

Leviticus 22:8. *He will never eat any animal that either dies on its own or is killed and torn apart by beasts, being made unclean by it. I am YHWH.*

Deuteronomy 14:21. *"You shall not eat of any thing that dies of itself: you shall give it unto the stranger that is in your gates, that he may eat it; or you may sell it unto an alien: for you are an holy people unto YHWH your Elohim. You shall not seethe a kid in his mother's milk."*

The commandment of not eating anything which dies of itself refers to death by natural means, regardless of how it died, it is forbidden to eat it. The commandment in Acts specifically states that the animal must not have died by strangulation, which is how some "un-kosher" butchers kill animals for food. In other words, the non-Jewish followers of Yeshua were commanded to take special precaution for where they obtained meat.

Imagine living in the days before Mashiyach, and bringing a sacrifice to the Temple to make restitution for wrong doing. Imagine taking an animal to Jerusalem for an offering during the celebration of a Feast. Treating the animal harshly, would reflect a negative attitude toward the forgiveness, grace and blessings being bestowed on you. Anyone who does not show kindness to animals, is not likely going to show kindness towards people!

The laws in Torah regarding animal welfare, are universal and timeless, because within the law are principles of Justice and Mercy that apply to all other components of life, even how we treat one another. Everything on our planet dovetails with laws that pertain to clean and unclean animals, and how we prepare our food, because they are part of YAHWEH's universal guidance.

The laws that pertain to animals show us that if we are to treat the blood of an animal with respect, how much more are we to respect human blood; how much more should we establish dignity for all people! There are many underlying laws and principles that enter in.

Exodus 34:14. "*For you shall worship no other god: for YHWH, whose name is Jealous, is a jealous Elohim: 15. Lest you make a covenant with the inhabitants of the land, and they go a whoring after their gods, and do sacrifice unto their gods, and one call thee, and you eat of his sacrifice; 16. And you take of their daughters unto thy sons, and their daughters go a whoring after their gods, and make thy sons go a whoring after their gods.*"

A very straightforward directive, but it doesn't bode well with a Church that is embarrassed by the absolutes of the Word of YAHWEH. Christian sons and daughters are being instructed to go whoring after pagan gods by their priests, pastors, fathers, and mothers who "see nothing wrong" with decorating Tammuz trees for Christ-Mass, painting Ishtar eggs that commemorates a sex goddess of fertility and celebrating their gods on Sun-day. This is the modern way of fractionalizing the Word of YAHWEH and "eating things" sacrificed to idols.

Abstaining from blood:

Leviticus 7:26. And you will never eat any form or kind of blood-- neither bird nor beast--in any of your dwellings. 27. Anyone who partakes of blood in any way, that person must be cut off from the midst of his people.

That's very clear and for the non-Jewish followers of Yeshua:

Leviticus 17:12. Therefore I said to the people of Israel, no one with you may eat blood, nor may any foreigner residing with you eat any blood.

When a person "stays away from blood", they are choosing to select meat that is butchered according to the Word of YAHWEH. When the Torah is looked at as a whole, and we can begin to understand the unity of the Word, we can easily deduce how an animal is to be slaughtered.

Scriptures like Genesis 22:10 *"And Avraham stretched forth his hand, and took the knife to slay his son"* reveals a methodology of slaying a sacrifice. The same knife that Avraham was about to use on his own beloved son, will very shortly see its real intended purpose:

Genesis 22:13. And Abraham lifted up his eyes, and looked, and behold, behind him a ram caught in the thicket by his horns. And Abraham went and took the ram, and offered him up for a burnt-offering in the stead of his son.

Obviously this foreshadowed Mashiyach ben Yoseph (Messiah of Joseph), who is Yeshua; however none of us can begin to image how important that ram was to either Avraham, or his son Yitzak (Isaac)! The blood of that ram was given in exchange for his beloved son's blood; how very grateful and contrite Avraham was toward the life of that very precious ram!

This event holds insight for how we are to regard the life of an animal, whether for sacrifice, or for food. By showing respect for blood we are not only agreeing that blood is very important to YAHWEH, but that life itself is of supreme importance to the Giver of all Life!

Genesis 9:3. Every moving thing that lives shall be food for you; as the green herb have I given you all. 4. But flesh with the life, which is of the blood, you will not eat. 5. And surely your blood, the blood of your lives, will I require; at the hand of every beast will I require it; and at the hand of man, even at the hand of every man's brother, will I require the life of man. 6. Whoever sheds man's blood, by man shall his blood be shed: for in the image of Elohim.

NOTE: The above is the beginning of *kashrut*, or kosher dietary laws. The diet in Eden was simply to avoid the fruit of one tree. Now, here for the first time, we are told that animals are to be slaughtered with the blood fully drained. This does not mean that Noah and Family can do this with pigs and shellfish. If we recall that Moses wrote both Genesis and Exodus we can defer to the great master to get more specific as he continues on with his narrative and explains that the banned animals never counted as "food" per se anyway.

Yes, staying away from blood is a "negative" don't do commandment, but the positive proactive command then is to honor the life of all living creatures!

In light of the commandment to stay away from blood, the commandment to "stay away from a strangled thing" has a new progressive meaning attached to it. A strangled thing could either mean that the animal was strangled to death before it was slaughtered, or it got strangled in a fence or in a natural setting. Either way, the animal did not die peacefully and the blood was not drained thoroughly.

The fact of the matter is that if the life of the animal is respected, then it is possible to slaughter it in a matter where it will die very peacefully, and not even know that it has been cut or that it is bleeding. For many, this is a difficult thing to contemplate, but of course we are not addressing vegetarians per se, but those who buy their meats from the guy across town. All who follow Yeshua, and who REALLY appreciate those summer barbecues in the park, or at the beach are commanded to "stay away from a strangled thing", no if's, but's or maybe's; therefore, the action of fulfilling this commandment draws us together in Mashiyach. Those who would defy this commandment are diverging from the Kingdom of Elohim, and the values that Mashiyach upheld with his own life!

When preparing the animal for slaughter, a person is to have a mindset that is consistent with regard to the blood of the animal. The blood and the life of the animal are synonymous, therefore the one doing the slaughter is to have an appreciation for the life he is taking, and show kindness toward the animal.

Acts 15: Does it really show that Christians don't need to be circumcised?

Many Christian leaders attempt to cite Acts 15:22-35 as proof that circumcision is only for the Jews. These leaders need to re-read the words of YAHWEH in Genesis 17 which clearly command non-Jews who are part of Isra'el to be circumcised:

Genesis 17:11. And you will be circumcised in the flesh of your foreskin. And it shall be a token of a covenant between me and you. 12. And he that is eight days old shall be circumcised among you, every male throughout your generations, he that is born in the house, or bought with money of any foreigner that is not of your seed. 13. He that is born in your house, and he that is bought with your money, must be circumcised. And my covenant shall be in your flesh for an everlasting covenant. 14. And the uncircumcised male who is not circumcised in the flesh of his foreskin, that soul shall be cut off from his people. He has broken my covenant.

A footnote in the Aramaic English New Testament explains that in Acts 15:28-29 we can see an example of binding and loosing: "The matter of circumcision was being applied commensurate to immediate need, as directed by the Ruach haKodesh (Holy Spirit). Instead of performing the act of circumcision before learning Torah, new converts are required to learn and apply Torah first, and then, when they have a good understanding, they are circumcised, but not the other way around. The keys of the Kingdom are wisdom and discernment given by the *Ruach haKodesh* to apply the Word of YAHWEH."

Yeshua, the Torah observant Jew who came to teach the world about YAHWEH and His Commandments, "bought and paid" for everyone including Gentiles with His own precious blood. Yeshua Himself was circumcised; therefore it stands to reason that anyone who believes in Him must also be circumcised.

Questions for Chapter 7

After reading Chapter 7 (and referring to your Bible), you should be able to answer the following questions. You may then compare your answers with those in the Appendix:

Question 1: After reading the beginning of Chapter 7, do you believe Acts 15 exempts Gentiles from being Torah observant? Why or why not?

Question 2: Should believing Gentiles be circumcised? Why or why not?

Question 3: Do you believe Paul's teachings contradict the teachings of Yeshua – even though Paul was a Torah observant Jew who said that the Law was NOT abolished but, rather, "established"?

Question 4: Please consult your Bible for this question: What did the woman with the issue of blood in Matthew 9:20-22 touch, and why?

Question 5: After having nearly completed this workbook and knowing what you now know, please write in your own words, why you think Christians are ignoring the Biblical Feasts and the seventh day Sabbath commands (especially since YAHWEH said His Sabbath is a "sign between Him and His people" – Ezekiel 20:12), and why Christians insist YAHWEH changed His mind about "clean" and "unclean" foods.

Question 6: Christians are guilty of "adding to" Scripture by coining new terms such as "Trinity" and "Rapture" and celebrating the man-made "holy days" of Christmas and Easter – none of which can be found in the Bible. Can you find any scriptures whatsoever that command us to celebrate the birth or resurrection of the Messiah via the man-made "holy days" of Christmas and Easter? What's more, is it okay to lie to your children about the existence of Santa Claus and egg-laying rabbits? What do these things have to do with Yeshua's birth and death and His purpose for coming?

Question 7: According to Joel 2:32 and Acts 2:21, those who are saved will do what?

Chapter 8

Do you still believe the "Law is a curse"?

*Deuteronomy 4:39. Know today and re-affirm the idea in your innermost being that YHWH is the Elohim of heaven above and the earth below and there is no other. 40. **Therefore, you are to keep His statutes and Mitzvot** (Commandments) which I am giving you today, in order that your days may be pleasant for yourself and for your children with you, that you may live long and well in the land that YHWH your Elohim is giving you for all time.*

Whenever you see the word "therefore" it often means something very important is to follow – which happens to be the case in verse 40 where we are told, *"you are to keep his laws and mitzvot (commands)....so that it will go well with you and with your children after you...."* In other words: Those who worship the God of Abraham, Isaac and Jacob **must** be Torah observant!

At the risk of being redundant, YAHWEH wasn't "cursing" man when He told Moses to present the Divine commandments for His people to live by! The commandments contained within Torah taught man right from wrong and showed us how to obey God and worship Him properly.

The "curse of the Law" is not the keeping of YAHWEH's Torah; it is our attempt to obtain salvation by following the law without faith because, as human beings, we are prone to stumble and fail at some point. ALL of His command-ments were given for a reason; ALL of them were given for our benefit. He didn't, after the Creation, throw Man out into a pasture to fend for himself; He gave us a divine blueprint for holy living.

Yet many Christians refuse to even bother with the Ten Commandments, let alone the "613", insisting "Jesus gave us just two to follow":

*Matthew 22:37. And Y'shua said to him, that "You should love Master YHWH your Elohim with all your heart and with all your soul and with all your might and with all your mind." 38. This is the first and the greatest Commandment. 39. And the second is like it. That "You should love your neighbor as yourself." 40. **On these two commandments hang Torah and the prophets.***

Please note and contemplate verse 40: Does it say you can now **ignore** the Law and the Prophets? Does this in any way suggest all other commands are now null and void? If those are the only two commandments to follow, the question remains: How do we know not to lie, murder, steal, commit adultery, etc.? From our parents? Our friends? Whom? And where did they find out how to behave in a Godly manner? The answer is: YAHWEH was the first One to present the rules of moral, Godly conduct – and there were certainly **more than two rules of conduct**! He graced us with many, revealing them according to His own desires and in His own good timing – and He expected them to be followed without question!

Ask anyone on the street to cite the Ten Commandments – or even just the "two" and see what happens. You will surely be hard-pressed to find even one who could provide a straight answer. Our society's absence of morality and penchant for "tolerance" and "acceptance" of ungodly behavior is ample evidence of that fact!

Matthew 22:37-40, read in context, means that if we love God with all our hearts, we will do whatever it takes to follow His Torah. According to the AENT:

> "The Torah and Prophets hang or 'hold on by' these two great commandments of Love. Those who do the Commandments, are they who love YAHWEH (Matt 19:17; 1 John 5:2-3). Without love, observance of Torah is vanity, and without Torah, one's 'love' is vanity."

Without YAHWEH's divine instructions, Man is totally lost! There were and are and always will be parts of Torah which God said would endure FOREVER....

2 Timothy 3:16. ***All Scripture*** *that was written by the Spirit is profitable for instruction and for decisive refutation, and for correction, and for deep extensive learning in righteousness; 17.* ***that the man of Elohim may become perfect and complete*** *for every good work.*

This verse from the *Brit Chadasha* (New Testament) says "ALL scripture is God-breathed"; it doesn't say, "All scripture except for the Torah...."

The *Tanakh* ("Old Testament") shows over and over that, in Biblical times, if a Gentile joined him or herself to Isra'el, they were required to give up their former pagan ways. The Bible states that there is **one** Torah for Isra'el and the Gentile who dwells with her. YAHWEH explicitly said:

Exodus 12:49. This same torah-instruction is to come to pass equally for your native-born as well for the foreigner who is living with you.

NOTE: Exodus 12:49 refers to "torah" with a small "t" meaning "instruction/command" as opposed to "Torah" with a big "T" which refers to a technical term for the entire moral code given at Sinai.

In other words: As believers in the God of Abraham, Isaac and Jacob, we are **one** in God's eyes, and are therefore required to act accordingly.

Leviticus 17:8. And then say to them, "If anyone from the household of Israel or from among the foreigners living with them brings forth an offering or a burnt sacrifice and does not bring it to the entrance of the tent of meeting as a sacrifice for YHWH, that person is to be cut off from his people."

Numbers 9:14. And if a foreigner is residing with you in your midst and wants to do the Passover unto YHWH, aligning with the regulations and requirements for Pesach for YHWH, thus shall he perform it [as you would]. You shall have one standard of conduct for the foreigner as for the native born of the Land.

Deuteronomy 31:12. Gather the people together as an assembly—the men, the women and the children—along with the foreigners that are residing with you in your towns— 13. so that they may hear, do, learn and understand the majesty of YHWH your Elohim, for as long as you dwell in the land that you are crossing over to the other side of the Yarden to take possession of.

Something to think about:

Deuteronomy 32:21. They have made me jealous with their non-existent gods and provoked me into wrath with their divine nothings, so that I will then provoke them into wrath with a foolish nation.

In the *Tanakh* the words "gentile", "heathen" and "pagan" were often synonymous. A Gentile was (and still is) a non-Jew, someone who did/does not believe in, or worship YAHWEH. (Please see Ezra 6:21, Nehemiah 5:8-9, Isaiah 9:1, 42:6.)

Romans 10:19. But I say: Did not Israel know? First, Moshe said thus: I will awaken your emulation by a people which is not a people; and by a disobedient people I will provoke you.

Those who are a "non-nation" are Gentiles, not Christians! Christians aren't a "nation"….

Romans 11:11. But I say: Have they so stumbled as to fall entirely? May it never be! Rather, by their stumbling, life has come to the Gentiles for (awakening) their jealousy.

Please note Paul, a Jew, does not say "Christians" or "the Church" will be grafted in or provoke Jews to jealousy; he said "Gentiles." In other words, it won't be the Christians through one of their myriad Torah-less denominations who end up making the Jews jealous; it will be the Torah observant believers in Messiah….

Zechariah 8:23. YHWH Tsavaot [of Hosts] says this: In those days, ten men from all the Nations will tenaciously grab at the winged edges of the garment of a Jew and say, May we please walk with you because we have heard that Elohim is in your midst.

Gentiles are "grafted in" to the Olive Tree. It's the Hebrews (now referred to as Jews) – the ones with whom YAHWEH made His original covenant – who are doing the sharing of the "rich root of the olive tree," not the Gentiles. However, the Torah observant Gentile believers in Messiah will certainly get to play a major part:

Romans 11:17. And if some of the branches were plucked off; and you, an olive from the desert, were in-grafted in their place and have become an heir of the root and fatness of the olive tree; 18. Do not boast over the branches. For if you boast, you do not sustain the root, but the root sustains you.

So, if anyone will lead the Jews to jealousy, it's those who are Torah observant believers in Yeshua Mashiyach – those who have put away their weak flesh and drawn close to YAHWEH and His Messiah by actually "walking out" God's will. Those who insist this is being "legalistic" don't realize **they** are the ones who have misunderstood the concept, because the Bible, over and over again, refers to our need to be Torah observant which has **nothing whatsoever** to do with "legalism":

*Joshua 1:8. Do not let this **Book of the Law** depart from your mouth; meditate on it day and night, so that you may be careful to **do everything written in it**. Then you will be prosperous and successful.*

As has been reiterated over and over again in this workbook, Yeshua was a Torah observant, Sabbath and feast-keeping, kosher Jew who was foreshadowed throughout the *Tanakh* and came to be our final **Sin** Sacrifice. To try to separate Him from His Jewishness makes about as much sense as separating Martin Luther King from his African-American heritage!

Genesis 49:10. The scepter shall not depart from Judah, nor the ruler's staff from between his feet, until Shiloh come. And to him shall the obedience of the peoples be.

Although this whole concept is certainly a hard pill to swallow for those God-fearing Christians who love the Lord with all their hearts, you must ask yourself this: Why would the Jews want to drop Torah and everything they've ever believed of their *Tanakh* in order to follow (the Christian) "Jesus" who in no way resembles the God of Abraham, Isaac and Jacob?

Yeshua Himself commanded us to spread the Gospel (Matthew 28:18) and Rav Sha'ul (Apostle Paul) later spoke of the Gentiles making the Jews "jealous" (Romans 10:19, 11:11 and 11:14 – which fulfilled Deuteronomy 32:21). We **must** spread the Good News; but we must do it according to YAHWEH's commands!

Although there are already many Jews whose spiritual eyes have been opened to the Truth of Messiah, the eyes of most traditional Jews are still blinded for now (but not for much longer because, judging from world events, especially in the Middle East, we are in the end times as outlined in the Books of Daniel and Revelation). YAHWEH scattered His chosen people for the purpose of spreading the word about Himself. If it hadn't been for the believing Jews, the world would **never** have heard of YAHWEH or Yeshua! He would have remained the best-kept secret of tiny, little Isra'el, and the rest of the world would still be drowning in paganism, unaware of the Torah or the Messiah.

Keeping in mind everything you've read here; please remember that in spreading the Gospel it is an absolute death knell to approach traditional Jews with words like: *"Jesus loves you; He died for you and while He was at it, He nailed the law to the cross so you don't have to perform 'works' anymore – and if you don't believe this, you'll go to hell."*

Only YAHWEH Himself will decide who will or won't be in Heaven with Him! Why would Jews want to worship someone who seems to contradict the entire *Tanakh* and who supposedly superseded His own "forever" commands – and whose followers, the "Christians," have been killing Jews since time immemorial in an effort to force them to "accept Jesus into their hearts"?

Furthermore, please ask yourself this: Why would Jews "believe in" a man who was apparently presented as a *human* sacrifice – as YAHWEH never demanded human sacrifices? If you will remember, He even sent a ram in the moments before Abraham was attempting to sacrifice his son, Isaac (Genesis 22:1-24). Most traditional Jews don't yet recognize that Yeshua – who came to *proclaim the Kingdom of* YAHWEH – was "an arm" (extension) of YAHWEH. He was a "man", but with a Divine Nature who ultimately **chose to martyr Himself** on our behalf.... His "sacrifice" was figurative and "He" did not die! We really should not say to a Jew: "...He died for you...", as it does not mean the same to them as intended!

Yeshua even spoke of the Kingdom (meaning YAHWEH and His Torah) *after* His death (Matthew 28:18-20, Mark 16:15-20, Luke 24:25-53)! Yeshua never once spoke of "the Gospels" or suggested that "grace" would somehow replace all of YAHWEH's divine Instructions in Righteousness. He *constantly* upheld Torah.

*Acts 1:3. Those who also to whom he revealed himself alive after he had suffered. With numerous signs for forty days he was being seen by them, and **he spoke concerning the Kingdom of Elohim**.*

Here's another fact: In perusing the Gospels we never see Yeshua perform any miracles *before* He was baptized, which knocks a hole in the "trinity" concept. Acts 10:37 - 38 tells us that when Yeshua was baptized, the power of YAHWEH came upon him and only *then* did He go about casting out devils, healing the sick, and other miracles. He simply didn't have the power of YAHWEH in his life until he was baptized, because He wasn't anointed of YAHWEH until He was baptized! As a man (even though He was the Son) Yeshua could do nothing on his own (John 5:30). It was the power of YAHWEH the Father who worked each and every one of the miracles through His Son.

Yeshua even said of himself that he was a man:

*John 8:40. But now behold, you seek to kill me, a **man** who truthfully spoke with you that which I heard from Elohim....*

*Acts 10:37. And also (you) know you about the word that was in all of Yehuda that went out from **Galeela after the immersion that Yochanan preached** 38. concerning Y'shua who was from Nasrath, that Elohim anointed with the Ruach haKodesh and with power. And this is he who traveled around and healed those who were oppressed by evil, because Elohim was with him. 39. And we (are)* *his witnesses concerning everything that he did in all the land of Yehud and of Urishlim. Him, this same one the Yehudeans hung upon wood and killed him. 40. **And Elohim raised him on the third day and allowed him to be seen openly.** 41. But not to all people, but to us, those who were chosen by Elohim to be witnesses for him. For we ate and drank with him after his resurrection from the dead.*

Yeshua was announced as Messiah, just as he was also called at some point in his ministry the King of Kings; but He did not step into those offices at the time of the announcements.

But yet many Christians – instead of educating themselves about the God of Abraham, Isaac and Jacob BEFORE opening their mouths – attempt to shove a non-Jewish, Torah-less "Jesus" down the world's collective throat while making ignorant comments about "the Jews." Cases in point: A well-known evangelist recently suggested that in the end of days Jews will eventually become "Christians"; while a well-known and popular author commented that the U.S. would be a better place if there weren't any Jewish people and that they needed to "perfect" themselves by becoming Christians.

Both comments stem from complete ignorance! Jews will never "become Christians" and the U.S. has been blessed, in part, **because** of the presence of YAHWEH's "Chosen People." While most Jews haven't yet realized that their promised Messiah has already come and will soon return, they do know who "God" is and they know He has promised that He will always take care of them:

Jeremiah 31:33. (Verse 34 in some versions) ...for I will forgive their depravity and remember their sin no more. 34. And YHWH also says: Who gives the sun for a light by day and the ordinances of the moon and of the stars as a light for the night? Who divides and stirs up the sea into thunderous waves? YHWH Tsavaot {of Hosts} is His Name!

151

Religious Jews are Torah observant and doing His will already – which certainly puts them in a favorable light with Him! But so far, they haven't been willing to acknowledge they already have a Final Sin Sacrifice in Yeshua. However, the Bible tells us they **will** one day:

Romans 11:25. (For I want you to know this) mystery, that blindness of heart has in some measure befallen Israel until the fullness of the Gentiles will come in: 26. And then will all Israel live. As it is written: A deliverer will come from Tsiyon and will turn away iniquity from Ya'akov. 27. And then will they have the covenant that proceed from me when I will have forgiven their sins.

"All Israel" refers to those who turn to YAHWEH and welcome the Spirit of Mashiyach. Paul does not say or mean that every Jew or Israelite by race will enter into the Kingdom of Elohim (see Matthew 22:2-14; 25:1-12).

YAHWEH as our Creator can offer eternal life to anyone He wants, and so no human has a right to decide who will or will not end up in heaven. In the meantime, believers must band together to show not only our Jewish brethren, but the entire world that Yeshua said **no one** comes to the Father except through Him:

John 14:6. Y'shua said to him, I am the Way and the Truth and the Life. No man comes to the Father except by me.

The Apostle Paul settled the matter long ago when he said:

Romans 1: 16. For I am not ashamed of the Good News; for it is the power of Elohim to life, to all who believe in it; whether first they are of the Jews, or whether they are of the Gentiles.

Yeshua Himself told His disciples to spread the Good News:

Matthew 28:19. Go therefore make disciples of all nations, and immerse them in the name of the Father and of the Son and of the

Ruach haKodesh. 20. **And teach them to keep all that I have commanded you.** *And behold, I am with you all the days until the end of the world. Amen.*

The bottom line is, if you want to be a good steward of God's Word and you desire to witness to a lost world including your Jewish brethren, forget about what your pastor has been teaching you and see for yourself what the Bible actually says! Hopefully, now you can see why....

The prophet Micah asked: *"With what shall I come before YHWH and bow down to Elohim from on high?"* (Micah 6: 6)

If you're one of the few who has actually grasped the concept of Torah in your journey through this book, then the answer to this question is crystal clear: "My total obedience to Him and His Torah! No more excuses, no more willingness to follow man's ideology or theology, and no more paganism!"

Psalms 119:*33. Teach me, O YHWH, the path of Your statutes and I will guard it for its own sake. 34 Give me discernment and I will watch over and keep Your Torah-instruction and preserve it with all of my heart.*

As sad as it might sound, because of their refusal to accept Torah, Christian pastors have renounced being holy and "Set Apart" unto YAHWEH, as this requires following in the footsteps of Mashiyach who led by example to show us how to do it.

To most Christians being "holy" means to be embedded in a church where belief in their particular theology is required (in most churches you can't become a member unless you sign an agreement that you adhere to their theology) and to join in whatever that church is doing to "win souls" and help it grow to enormous proportions by perpetuating "ear tickling" doctrine. Is this really what you want to offer YAHWEH on Judgment Day – to tell Him, "Lord, I did all this for You"? Or would you rather be able to stand before Him and proclaim: "Abba Father, I did it Your way!"

*Matthew 7:21. It will not be that just anyone who says to me "My master, my master." Will enter the Kingdom of Heaven, but **whoever does the will of my Father who is in heaven.** 22. Many will say to me in that day, "My master, my master. By your name, have we not prophesied? And by you name have we cast out demons? And by your name have we done many miracles?" 23. And then I will profess to them that from everlasting, I have not known you. Depart from me, you workers of iniquity!*

A word of warning: IF, you are among the few who has fully grasped the concept of Torah, and IF, as a result, you decide to become Torah observant, be prepared for some major persecution from those who cannot or will not see. It has been my experience that most Christians will fight you to the death over the idea of "the law". Once the persecution comes, all you can do is to cling to the Word and ask yourself: "Whom will I follow – God or man and mammon?" In those trying times it will be imperative to remember the words of Yeshua who said:

Matthew 10:21. And brother will deliver his brother to death, and a father his son. And children will rise up against their parents and kill them. 22. And you will be hated by all men because of my name, but whoever that endures until the end, he will live.

Matthew 10:34. Do not think that I have come to bring calm on earth. I have not come to bring calm, rather a sword. 35. For I have come to divide a man from his father, and a girl from her mother. And a daughter-in-law from her mother-in-law. 36. And the adversaries of a man will be his household.

Matthew 10:37. Whoever loves father or mother more than me is not worthy of me. And whoever loves son or daughter more than me is not worthy of me. 38. And anyone that does not take up his staff and come and follow me is not worthy of me. 39. Whoever finds his soul will lose it, and whoever loses his soul for my sake will find it.

Some final thoughts:

Zechariah 13:4. And it will come to pass that in that time, each one of the prophets will be ashamed by his vision when he prophesies and he will not put on a cloak of hair to deceive people. 5. Instead he will say, I am not prophet but merely a tiller of soil since a man had sold me into slavery when I was a young boy. 6. Then if someone asks him, Then what are these deep cuts between your shoulders? He will answer, I got those when I was wounded in the house of my friends. 7. Awake O sword, against my shepherd and against the man and against my close companion, says YHWH Tsavaot! Strike the shepherd and the sheep will be scattered; and I will turn My hand against the small youths. 8. In time, throughout that land, says YHWH, two thirds of those who live there will die but the last third will remain. 9. That third part I will refine them in the same way as silver and their tests will be the same as the tests for gold. They will call on My Name and I will answer them by saying, This is My people, and they will say, YHWH is my Elohim.

Notice that two parts get wiped out and then the third part goes through the Refiner! Are **you** ready? Or are you going to keep worshipping YAHWEH according to the ways of Man? Mashiyach **Yeshua brought a government, not a religion** and many will come to realize in these latter days that His Government will test, try and shake out everything that is not of YAHWEH. My prayer for all of you is that you would drop all man-made ideas and begin to follow the One who created you!

Romans 7:7. What will we say then? Is Torah sin? May it never be! For I had not learned sin except by means of Torah: for I had not known lust, had not Torah said, You will not covet: 8. And by this Commandment sin found occasion and perfected in me all lust: for without Torah, sin was dead.

Romans 7:12. As a result, Torah is Set Apart (holy); and the Commandment is Set Apart, and righteous, and good.

The following is from an article entitled, "The Sanctuary or the Church" at Mashiyach.com, used with permission:

> The fact of the matter is that Christian Pastors have NO Fear of YAHWEH; they've been trained according to a pagan hierarchy to fear man, and climb the Christo-political ladder. The Seminary gave them "credentials" and "better doctrine" than other denominations, so with the backing of some "reformer" or institution, who needs the real Mashiyach? As long as people keep coming back every Sunday or Sabbath, the Pastor feels he must be doing something right.
>
> Christians who actually read their Bibles and are honest with themselves, already know that the Church is on the other side of a great gulf. It's nearly impossible to bridge the gulf between the Kingdom of Elohim and false religious traditions because the church is so deeply entrenched into a pagan value system, culture and government that breaks Torah.
>
> … One of the most famous sayings of Pastors is, "it's not for today", or "Yes, I would love to enjoy Shabbat" or "Yes, the Feasts are awesome" but yet they put up their Tammuz trees, and paint their Ishtar eggs, because people will leave their churches if they are not given that old time Christian religion. Gutless pastors are the vast majority; they are hirelings who lead an apostate fallen religious system that plagues the earth….
>
> Why would anyone want to put their trust in any other than Mashiyach? What a foolish game to play when people look to their Rabbi or Pastor or Guru as a hero of truth. YAHWEH warned us through John to "come

out of her my people" and he wasn't talking about the bingo halls! It is very clear about the Testimony of Yeshua, "Blessed are they that do His commandments, that they may have right to the Tree of Life, and may enter in through the gates into the city. For without are dogs, and sorcerers, and whoremongers, and murderers, and idolaters, and whosoever loves and makes a lie."

I pray the words of this book have caused you to rethink what you have been taught in your churches. Although I already used this in a previous chapter, I want to close with these thoughts from Andrew Gabriel Roth, which beautifully sum up the whole idea behind, "Should Christians be Torah Observant?"... specifically answering the question as to what was nailed to the cross:

"So when we are guilty of sin, YAHWEH is one witness to that guilt, and the record that is generated of that sin is another. However, with the reconcilement of Y'shua on the cross dying in our place, that second witness/record against us is obliterated, and the Torah remains simply to guide us in the path of right- eousness for the rest of our redeemed lives."

Questions for Chapter 8

After reading Chapter 8 (and referring to your Bible), you should be able to answer the following questions. You may then compare your answers with those in the Appendix:

Question 1: After having finished all eight chapters of this workbook, do you still feel that "the law is a curse? Why or why not?

Question 2: What, exactly, is the "curse of the Law"?

Question 3: Matthew 5:19 says: *"All who loosen, therefore, from one (of) these small commandments and teach thus to the sons of man, will be called little in the Kingdom of Heaven, but all who do and teach this will be called great in the Kingdom of Heaven."* This passage seems to indicate a hierarchy in heaven showing that those who teach against Torah will be relegated to a much lesser status. How, then, can Christianity justify that Torah has been abolished?

Question 4: Matthew 7:21-23 discusses how YAHWEH will reject the "workers of lawlessness." Who are the "workers of lawlessness"?

Question 5: Please read Matthew 22:37-40. Do these verses in any way suggest the other many commands are now null and void?

Question 6: Many Christians insist they don't have to bother with those "Old Testament commands" because "Jesus has written the law on our hearts." Without referring to the Bible, can you name at least five of the Ten Commandments?

Question 7: Second Timothy 3:16-17 says: *All Scripture that was written by the Spirit is profitable for instruction and for decisive refutation, and for correction, and for deep extensive learning in righteousness; that the man of Elohim may become perfect and complete for every good work.* Do you believe "all scripture" includes the "Old Testament" scriptures as well? Why or why not?

Question 8: Please read Romans 11:11 and write down exactly who will end up causing the Jews to become "jealous" and why.

Question 9: In view of the above, do you think it's a good idea to tell a Jewish person they will go to hell if they don't believe in Jesus? Why or why not?

Question 10: The prophet Micah asked: "With what shall I come before YAHWEH and bow down to Elohim from on high?" (Micah 6:6) What should your answer be?

Question 11: At this point in your studies you should recognize the fact that the original followers of Yeshua and His disciples were all Torah observant and that Christianity was borne out of Catholicism which had totally twisted the teachings of Yeshua. That being the case, how can today's Christians claim that their respective churches are the "original church that Jesus built" when none of them observe Torah, and most of them ignore the seventh day Sabbath and the Biblical feasts? Does your church in any way resemble anything that Yeshua originally taught? Please check the Bible thoroughly before answering.

Question 12: If you are among the few fully grasping the concept of Torah and, **if** as a result, you decide to become Torah observant, be prepared for some major persecution from those who cannot or will not see. Many, if not most, Christians will fight you to the death over the idea of "the law". Once the persecution comes, all you can do is to cling to the Word and ask yourself: "Whom will I follow – God or mammon?" After reading this workbook, what will your answer be?

Epilogue

A quick review of what you've learned....

Many (if not most) Christians insist: "God is love and that's all we need to know. He sent His Son to die for us, and Jesus will protect us because His laws are written on our hearts, and nothing else matters." So here's a hypothetical scenario:

A father teaches his child not to cross the road unless he has looked both ways; he did that because he LOVES the child. The child, believing that the father's love is all encompassing, doesn't bother to continue to obey what the father **said** because, hey, "Dad is LOVE, and he won't let anything happen to me!" So, the kid just goes ahead and crosses the road without looking – and, consequently, gets smashed by a semi-truck.

So, how did the father's **love** save that child? Love can only go so far before responsibility kicks in! There are certain rules the child should have obeyed in order to please his father and continue living with and FOR the father. Loving God includes obeying His rules because they are our **only** blueprint for moral, holy living!

If you wish to insist that Torah has been abolished along with "all that Old Testament stuff," you have also abolished the Ten Commandments because they, too, are "Old Testament." (Ask your pastor why he believes the command to tithe is still valid, since tithing was commanded in the "Old Testament"!)

Yeshua Himself conducted His life by obeying and carrying out His Father's Divine Instructions/Commands! He was completely Torah observant, as were all of His apostles and disciples throughout the entire First Century....so what makes Christians think they don't have to be?

Why is it that most Christians never ask themselves exactly **how** Yeshua's death supposedly negated His Father's Divine Instructions in Righteousness? Why don't they ever ask themselves **how and why** YAHWEH's Divine Instructions got to be a "curse"? Why don't they ever ask themselves why the Apostles bothered to teach Torah at all if it was supposed to be abolished after Messiah's death:

1 John 2:3. And by this we will be sensible that we know him, if we keep his Commandments. 4. For he that says I know him, and does not keep his Commandments, is a liar and the truth is not in him. 5. But he that keeps his Word, in him is the Love of Elohim truly completed: for by this we know that we are in him. 6. He that says I am in him, is bound to walk according to his halacha (religious law).

The above, in itself, reveals there must be more to God and the Bible than just "believing in Jesus" and it's **way** past time for mankind to realize this. We are in the end times as outlined in the Books of Daniel and Revelation, and it won't be much longer before Yeshua's return. Those who have chosen to ignore God's Torah are NOT worshiping the God of Abraham, Isaac and Jacob, and they will be very surprised to discover they were "left behind" on that fateful day when "the rapture" happens, because – whether they know it or not – they were guilty of being "lukewarm."

Many of our Christian brethren have already realized this and opted to leave the "milk" of the church in order to pursue a true relationship with their Creator because they've finally understood that Yeshua said He did NOT come to abolish or negate His Father's Commands:

Matthew 5:17. Do not think that I have come to loosen Torah or the prophets, I have not come to loosen but to fulfill. 18. For truly I say to you that until heaven and earth pass away not one Yodh or one stroke will pass from Torah until everything happens. 19. All who loosen, therefore, from one (of) these small commandments and teach thus to the sons of man, will be called little in the Kingdom of Heaven, but all who do and teach this will be called great in the Kingdom of Heaven. 20. For I say to you that unless your righteousness exceeds more than that of the scribes and the Pharisees, you will not enter the Kingdom of Heaven.

Has everything happened that must happen? Have heaven and Earth passed away? Since when does the word "complete" (or "fulfill") mean "abolished"? Why would

God abolish His own original divine instructions in righteousness which He said were to last forever? Did Jesus come to make a liar out of His Father?

Regardless, mainstream Christianity insists "Jesus" preached the Gospel - the Good News about the Messiah's death, burial, and resurrection, which is all they tend to focus on. But the Scriptures, read in context, reveal He did **not** preach those things at all; rather, He preached the Kingdom of YAHWEH!

Luke 4:43. And Y'shua said to them that, it is necessary for me to preach to other cities the Kingdom of Elohim, for because this reason I have been sent.

Acts 24:14. But this indeed I (Paul) acknowledge, that in that same doctrine of which they speak, I do serve the Elohim of my fathers, believing all the things written in Torah and in the prophets.

Acts 28:23. And they appointed him (Paul) a day; and many assembled, and came to him at his lodgings. And he explained to them respecting the Kingdom of Elohim, testifying and persuading them concerning Y'shua, out of the Torah of Moshe, and out of the prophets, from morning till evening.

While Yeshua's death, burial, and resurrection are an important part of the Good News, it's not the whole story! God isn't just in the business of "saving" people; as Creator and law giver, He is in the business of teaching us how to be good subjects in His Kingdom to come! If "Jesus abolished Torah at the cross" then why was **every** believer completely Torah observant for approximately one hundred years after Yeshua's death, including the Apostle Paul who was "caught" being Torah observant 29 years after Yeshua's death (Acts 21:23-24)? Was Paul a hypocrite, saying one thing and doing another; or were his teachings, perhaps, just a wee bit misunderstood?

But Romans 10:4 tells us that Christ is the "end of the Law!"

No, it doesn't. That is just another gross mistranslation from the Greek! The following was borrowed from an appendix from Andrew Gabriel Roth's Aramaic English New Testament:

Here is an important and very beautiful phrase that is equally apparent in both Aramaic and in Greek:

"Mashiyach is the end (Gk. *telos) of the Torah, so that there may be righteousness for everyone who believes."* Romans 10:4 (NIV)

While *telos* can mean "end" it is very irresponsible to render it this way due to the flexibility of that term in the receiving language. In English, "end" has two meanings. The first is "termination" which is the majority usage of the word in English. However, we also have phrases such as "the ends do not justify the means." In this case, the lesser-used meaning is that of "goal" which applies in both Greek and English.

Rav Shaul clearly refers to the Torah itself as "perfect, righteous and good" (Romans 7:12), so it is very foolish to then think that he turns around and teaches the "termination" of Torah. Instead, and as Rav Shaul clearly teaches in Galatians 3, Torah is the tutor that instructs and brings people to Mashiyach. Then, when a person understands and accepts the fact that Y'shua is Mashiyach, he (Mashiyach) becomes Torah's goal. This is also one of the many meanings behind the cryptic remark in Yochanan 1, calling Y'shua the "Word (Torah) made flesh." By extreme contrast, the NIV translation of Romans 10:4 is the exact opposite of what the original texts meant! NIV makes it sound like Rav Shaul is a train conductor calling out a stop—"End of the Torah! Everyone get off!"

Furthermore, in certain key Renewed Covenant passages, *telos* can only mean "goal":

"But now that you have been set free from sin and have become slaves to Elohim, the benefit you reap leads to holiness, and the goal (telos) is eternal life." Romans 6:22

"The goal (telos) of this command is love, which comes from a pure heart and a good conscience and a sincere faith." I Timothy 1:5

"Obtaining as the goal (telos) of your faith the salvation for your souls." 1 Peter 1:9

In Aramaic we find these same verses have the same reading as "goal" with the word *saka*. Like *telos*, the context provides the key to realizing the intended meaning. Because Rav Shaul continually upholds Torah in every way (Romans 3:31), then "goal" is also very consistent with the rest of his teaching.

Here's the thing: The "Old Testament" is YAHWEH's Word; The "New Testament" is *about* God's Word. One can be "saved" by believing in the Messiah (the "arm of YAHWEH" – Isaiah 53), but one cannot possibly understand God until one is firmly rooted in Torah.

Isaiah 53:1. Who has believed our report and to whom has the arm of YHWH been revealed?

Seemingly forgetting that "Jesus" was the **Son**, sent by YAHWEH, Christianity has pushed our Creator into the background and insisted that Jesus has somehow usurped all of God's power and "nailed to the cross" all of His Torah (1 Corinthians 11: 3). Not only that, but they changed the Messiah's name along with the dates of His birth, death and resurrection, and removed all traces of His Jewishness. As a matter of fact, whenever we see Jesus hanging on some cross, he's often depicted as a blond, blue-eyed Adonis instead of the plain, Jewish man He was:

Isaiah 53:2. ...For he grew up before Him like a tender young plant and like a root out of parched ground. He has no great form or splendor that we should look upon him or handsomeness that we should find him attractive. 3. He was hated and rejected by men, a man of pain well acquainted with sickness. And like one from whom men hide their face he was completely hated and we did not even think of him.

Please read the following very carefully:

Yeshua (His given Hebrew Name which means, "YAHWEH is Salvation" while "Jesus" means nothing in particular), was a Torah observant Jew who kept all the Biblical Feasts and the Seventh Day Sabbath. Contrary to popular belief, He was not born on December 25th; He was born on the first day of Sukkot (Feast of Tabernacles) which always falls in the September/October time frame on our Gregorian calendars. His exact date of death according to the Bible was Nisan 14 (Passover) and He rose three days later on Saturday evening, not on a Sunday. (And even if He was resurrected on a Sunday morning, what did that have to do with, and how did it change YAHWEH's Seventh Day Sabbath?)

Besides the Seventh Day Sabbath, God gave us seven Feasts which He said believers were to keep forever, and Yeshua has so far only fulfilled the first four; yet Christians as a whole have chosen to ignore them and instead, celebrate their man-made "holy days" of Christmas and Easter - both of which are steeped in paganism, and something man was amply warned against, time and time again. Example:

Jeremiah 10:1. Hear the word which YHWH speaks to you, O house of Israel! 2. YHWH says this: Do not learn the way of the Nations and do not tremble with fear at the signs in the heavens that the Nations tremble at. 3. For the customs of the Nations are as a passing vapor—nothing! It is the artifice only of a craftsman who cuts down a tree in the forest with an axe. 4. He then decorates it with silver and gold and fastens it with hammer and nails so that it does not move. 5. They are like a scarecrow in a cucumber patch. They cannot speak! And they must be carried about because they cannot walk! Do not fear them because they can do neither good nor evil.

Ezekiel 8:13. And He said to me, Turn around again and you will see the great abominations that they practice. 14. Then He brought me to the entrance of the northern gate of YHWH's House (Temple) and right there in front me were women weeping for Tammuz! 15. Then He said to me, Have you seen this O son of Man (mortal man)? Turn back again and you will behold even greater abominations than these. 16. **Then He brought me to the inner court of YHWH's House— and behold!—at the door of the Temple of YHWH, between the porch and the altar, there were about twenty-five men with their backs to the Temple of YHWH and with their faces turned to the east as they worshipped the sun in the east!** *17. He asked me, have you seen this O son of Man? Is it a casual matter that the house of Yehudah that they practice the abominations that they do here and fill the land with violence and angering me even more? Behold! They are even putting the branch to their nose! 18. Therefore I will act with fury, My eye will spare no one and I will have no compassion. Even if they cry loudly in my ear I will refuse to listen to them.*

While these scriptures aren't referring to "Christmas trees" or "Easter Sunday" per se, they are a clear warning to stay away from customs like these. We need to remember that YAHWEH used to put people to death for gross disobedience....in essence, for worshipping Him with "strange fire":

Leviticus 10:1. But Nadav and Avihu, sons of Aaron, each took his censer and after putting fire in it also placed incense inside it and offered strange fire before YHWH, which YHWH had not commanded them to do. 2. Then fire went out from the presence of YHWH and consumed them, and they died before YHWH.

Many protest that Torah was "just for the Jews," but please think about this: Where did God ever say He was going to treat His adopted children any differently from His natural ones? Torah is our only blueprint for moral, holy and godly living! The **only** thing Yeshua "nailed to the cross" was the requirement to kill an innocent animal to atone for our sins, and that in no way negates the need for Torah!

Please think about this, too: Back when YAHWEH created the world and made the seventh day holy (Genesis 2:2-3), He wasn't talking to just "the Jews" because there were no Jews back then! (As a matter of fact, "Jews" became a blanket term for Israel way after Jacob begat the tribe of Judah.) Adam and Eve, to whom He gave His first rules weren't Jews, and neither were Cain and Abel who offered the first sin sacrifices. And Noah, who also was not a Jew, knew the difference between "clean and unclean" animals....

As you can see below, YAHWEH Himself said that anyone who wants to follow the God of Abraham, Isaac and Jacob is to be Torah observant:

*Numbers 15:13. **All who are native born** will do these things by this method, by presenting an offering by fire as a soothing aroma unto YHWH. 14. As for the rest in your assembly, there will **be one statute for you and the same statute for the foreigner living with you.** 15. This is an **eternal requirement throughout all your generations, that as you are so shall the foreigner be before YHWH.** 16. **The same instruction and judgment will apply equally to both you and the foreigner living with you.***

Please re-read the above in case you missed it: Any Torah-less non-Jew/Hebrew/Israelite who does not yet believe in the God of Abraham, Isaac and Jacob is an "alien"/foreigner. However, if they do wish to accept Him, then they are to do exactly as those who are already belong to Him!

"Living among" means not necessarily physically, but rather, it refers to all those who have accepted the God of Abraham, Isaac and Jacob. They MUST be Torah observant, just like the Houses of Israel and Judah were with whom God made His New Covenant (Jeremiah 31:32), which is reiterated and confirmed in Romans 10:

Jeremiah 31:31. Behold! The day is coming, says YHWH, when I will carve out a new covenant with the house of Israel and the house of Yehudah.

NOTE: The word *karet*, translated as "carve out" is not a general word "to make/create" per se like Genesis 1:1. It literally means "to cut out/cut away" but in English that can sometimes lead to the opposite meaning of "destroy". Nevertheless, in context "carve out" makes a lot more sense. The first covenant was carved out on the rock of Sinai and was literally broken with the worship of the Golden Calf before Moshe had even descended from the mountain. Then new tablets also had to be "carved out" to ratify the covenant again. Similarly, the prophet here is saying that Israel and Yehudah broke His covenant again, leading to another one being carved out.

Romans 10:12. And in this, it discriminates neither Jews nor Gentiles. For there is one, Master YHWH, over them all, who is abundantly generous towards every one that calls on him. 13. For everyone that will call on the name of Master YHWH, will have life.

It is very important to understand that YAHWEH did NOT make His New Covenant with the Gentiles; He made it with those who were obedient to His divine Instructions! Same God, same rules for both the "natural" and the "grafted-in" children, to whom He extended His grace and mercy once they become believers in Yeshua, and therefore automatically become part of "Israel"!

And God told Israel: *"I give you good instruction: Do not forsake my Torah"* (Proverbs 4:2). Paul reiterated this when he said: *Do, we then nullify Torah by faith? May it never be! On the contrary, we establish Torah.* (Romans 3:31).

Paul also wrote in Acts 21 - a full 29 years after the death of Yeshua:

Acts 21:25. As to those of the Gentiles who have believed, we have written, that they should keep themselves from (an idol's) sacrifice, and from sexual sin, and from what is strangled, and from blood." 26. Then Paul took those men, on the following day, and was purified with them; and he entered and went into the temple, explaining to them how to complete the days of the purification, up to the presentation of the offering by each of them.

This event clearly establishes Rav Shaul as a Torah observant Jew; however, most mainstream Christians twist Paul into being a man pleaser – as though his offering was solely to please Jews, as some sort of political posturing. There is no conflict between atonement made by Yeshua's blood and the giving of offerings in the Temple. Paul walks in the footsteps of Yeshua, King David, and all the Israel of Elohim when he *declares "I rejoice in the Torah of Elohim, in the inner man"* (Romans 7:22).

Paul wrote:

Romans 7:7. What will we say then? Is Torah sin? May it never be! For I had not learned sin except by means of Torah: for I had not known lust, had not Torah said, You will not covet: 8. And by this Commandment sin found occasion and perfected in me all lust: for without Torah, sin was dead.

Romans 7:12. As a result, Torah is Set Apart; and the Commandment is Set Apart, and righteous, and good.

Paul also said that Y<small>AHWEH</small>'s law is spiritual (Romans 7:14) - and that which is spiritual is eternal.

2 Corinthians 4:18. While we look not at these seen things, but at those not seen; for these seen things are temporary, but those not seen are eternal.

So, the question once more is: Why would Yeshua's death have abolished Torah? Those who teach contrary to the Torah, which both Yeshua and Paul upheld, are false preachers and prophets; nothing more, nothing less. Paul wrote:

2 Corinthians 11:13. For they are false apostles, crafty workers, and pretend apostles of the Mashiyach. 14. And in this there is nothing strange. For if Satan pretends to be a Messenger of light, 15. It is no great thing if his ministers pretend to be ministers of righteousness whose end will be according to their works.

And the prophet Micah said:

Micah 6:8. He has instructed you directly O Man on what is good, And what does YHWH demand of you except to do justice, love grace and walk humbly with your Elohim?

How do you walk in purity with God unless you are **obeying** Him?

The prophet Isaiah tried to warn us about man's stubbornness and arrogance and tendency to come up with his own rules:

Isaiah 29:9. Be slow thinking and remain paralyzed in the mind! Act blind and remain blinded. You are intoxicated, but not from strong drink. 10. The reason [for your paralysis] is because YHWH has poured over you a spirit of deep sleep. He has shut your eyes (who were) the prophets and covered you head (which was) the seers. 11. And whole of the vision shall be unto you like the words in a sealed scroll, which when they give it to one who has knowledge [of reading] and says, "Please read this", he answers, "I cannot because it is sealed". 12. If the scroll is then given to one who cannot read along with the request, "Please read this", he says, "I cannot read". 13. Then YHWH said, "Because this people draw near unto Me with their words and honor me with their lip service, yet they remove their hearts far from Me and their reverence for Me has turned into a man-made learned tradition, 14. therefore behold! I will once more deal with these people in utterly shocking ways—shocking beyond belief! For the wisdom of the wise will perish. And the understanding from those with discernment will be covered over in darkness. 15. Woe to those who bury down deep to conceal their counsel from YHWH and whose works are done in a dark place and then say "Who sees us?" and "Who knows us?" 16. How you pervert and turn things backwards! Will the potter be considered the same as the clay he shapes? Should that which is created say to its Creator, "He did not fashion me"? Or shall what is made say to its Maker, "He is ignorant"?

To truly please YAHWEH, we must first get to know Him, and getting to know Him includes studying and obeying the rules he laid down. He never gave us the leeway to ignore those rules! Yes, He gave us free will, but those who choose to accept Him as their God are bound by His rules. Loving God requires a lot more than just "believing in Jesus."

Appendix:

Answers to Questions

Chapter 1, Question 1: Have you ever read the Bible from cover to cover? If not, how much of it have you actually read?

Answer: This question was designed to get you to think about the amount of time you have actually spent studying the Scriptures. Many people have never read the Bible at all; the only time they bother to open it is when their pastors on Sunday mornings tell them to turn to a certain chapter and verse. Unfortunately, many have built their entire theology around this limited knowledge, never hungering for more or questioning their pastors about anything that is espoused in their churches.

Chapter 1, Question 2: According to the Scriptures, who is God and what is His Name?

Answer: "God" is just a title that can pertain to anyone, including mere humans. But the Creator of the universe actually has a Name that He revealed to Moshe (Moses):

Exodus 3:13. Moshe said to Elohim, "Look, when I appear before the people of Isra'el and say to them, 'The Elohim of your ancestors has sent me to you'; and they ask me, 'What is his name?' what am I to tell them?" 14. Elohim said to Moshe, "Ehyeh Asher Ehyeh [I am Who I am, I will be What I am]," and added, "Here is what to say to the people of Isra'el: 'Ehyeh [I Am or I Will Be] has sent me to you.'" 15. Elohim said then to Moshe, "Say this to the people of Isra'el: 'YAHWEH [He is], the Elohim of your fathers, the Elohim of Avraham, the Elohim of Yitz'chak and the Elohim of Ya'akov, has sent me to you.' This is my name for all time; this is how generation after generation is to remember Me."

173

YAHWEH is the name God revealed both to Abram in Genesis 13 and later to Moses in Exodus 3, יהוה (the Hebrew letters Yud-Hey-Vav-Hey = YHWH, pronounced YAH-WEH). These letters were inspired by the *Ruach haKodesh* (Holy Spirit) to appear nearly 7,000 times in the *Tanakh* (Old Testament), yet the Name is nowhere to be found in our English versions except where it appears in an abbreviated form at the end of the word "Halleluyah." English translators were guilty of adding to our Creator's Word by replacing His personal Name with the capital letters LORD, GOD and the hybrid "Jehovah". Ironically, Jews know His Name but they refuse to utter it for fear of mispronouncing or misspelling it....

Chapter 1, Question 3: Who was the Son and why was He sent?

Answer: He was an "arm of YAHWEH" (Isaiah 53:1); the Word of YAHWEH come-in-the-flesh to basically "put a face" on God and teach mankind about God and how to worship Him, and who then martyred Himself as the Final Sin Sacrifice. He even told us why He came! "And Y'shua said to them that, 'It is necessary for me to preach to other cities the Kingdom of Elohim, for because this reason I have been sent.'" (Luke 4:43). We can only gain eternal life through belief in Him (John 14:6).

Chapter 1, Question 4: Who was in charge of the universe while Yeshua was down here on earth?

Answer: YAHWEH was in charge then, and always has been! As mentioned above, His Son Yeshua was "an arm of YAHWEH" (Isaiah 53:1) who came in the form of a human being who was here temporarily to proclaim the Kingdom of YAHWEH (Luke 4:43). Yeshua, in human form, was YAHWEH's Divine Representative on earth. The "arm" cannot move without the will of the "brain" (or, in this case, YAHWEH Himself). As we can see in Bible verses such as the below, Yeshua, as a human, was limited as to what He could do:

*John 8:47. Y'shua said to them, Amen, amen I say to you that before Awraham existed, I was! 48. And they took up rocks to stone him, **and Y'shua hid and departed from the temple** and passed through their midst and left.*

Why would *God* have to hide in order to save Himself from humans? Yes, Yeshua had a divine Nature; but that does not negate the fact that He was still human, someone who could be hurt and even die on the day He was nailed to the stake! While YAHWEH (God) was in charge of the universe, His divine Representative was down here on earth, proclaiming the Kingdom and doing HIS will.

John 10:25. Y'shua answered and said to them, I have told you and you do not believe! And the works that I do in the Name of my Father they testify concerning me. 26. But you do not believe because you are not of my sheep, just as I have told you. 27. My sheep hear my voice and I know them and they come after me. 28. And I give to them life that is eternal and they will not perish and no man will ever snatch them from my hands. **29. For my Father who gave them to me is greater than all, and no man is able to snatch them from the hands of my Father. 30. I and the Father are one.** *31. And again the Yehudeans took up rocks to stone him.*

Let's take this a little further: Isaiah 53:1 says, "to whom has the arm of YHWH been revealed?" This is the only acceptable form of "Godhead" in Scripture. Clearly not a Trinity of three separate beings (or persons), because the arm is not a separate entity from the rest of the body and has no independent will. The "arm" moves only with the power and control from the mind. In the same way YAHWEH's nature is manifest as an occurrence within the Son that is separate but yet side-by-side with his human nature. These two natures then communicate with one another; thus explaining why Yeshua is not talking to himself when he prays to his Father. This fact is also why sometimes Yeshua says things like, "My teaching is not my own" and "I can do nothing without my Father" on the one hand but on the other he says, "If you have seen me, you have seen the Father" and "I and my Father are one of the same." This indicates a 100 percent divine nature that exists in a 100 percent human soul and flesh, where one (the Father) or the other (Yeshua) talks *through* Yeshua. But the human is subject to the divine (again, "Not my will...") which is the only way the Scripture cannot be broken. Yeshua is not part of a "trinity"; but neither does this deny the divine aspects in Yeshua himself. It is also the real meaning behind, "No one comes to the Father but by me." See also John 5:26.

Chapter 1, Question 5: What was Jesus' given, Hebrew Name and what does it mean?

Answer: YAHWEH's Son's given Hebrew Name was actually יׁשוע which, transliterated into English is Y'shua or Yeshua, which means "YAHWEH is

Salvation."

Chapter 1, Question 6: Was Yeshua a Jew or Gentile? How do you know?

Answer: Called "the Son of David" throughout the Gospels, we constantly see Yeshua presenting Himself as a Torah observant, *tallit*-wearing, Seventh Day Sabbath and Feast-keeping Jew who came through the line of Yehuda (Judah) through His mother Miriam (Mary). Follow the genealogy as provided in Matthew and Luke, being careful to note that one genealogy provides the royal line to King David, while the other provides the bloodline to King David. Thus we know Yeshua was a Jew (of the tribe of Yehuda), who carried the bloodline to be King:

Matthew 1:1. The book of the genealogy of Y'shua the Mashiyach, the son of Dawid, the son of Awraham. 2. Awraham fathered Yitz'chak, Yitz'chak fathered Ya'akov. Ya'akov fathered Yehuda and his brothers. 3. Yehuda fathered Peretz and Zarakh by Thamar. Peretz fathered Khetzron. 4. Khetzron fathered Aram. Aram fathered Amminadav, Amminadav fathered, Nekhshon. Nekhshon fathered Salmon. 5. Salmon fathered Bo'az by Rachav, Bo'az fathered Awbed by Rawth, Awbed fathered Ishai. 6. Ishai fathered Dawid the king. Dawid fathered Shlemon by the wife of Awrea. 7. Shlemon fathered Rechav'am, Rechav'am fathered Aviyah, Aviyah fathered Asa. 8. Asa fathered Yahoshapat, Yahoshapat fathered Yoram, Yoram fathered Uziyahu. 9. Uziyahu fathered Yotham, Yotham fathered Akhaz, Akhaz fathered Hizkiyahu. 10. Hizkiyahu fathered M'nasheh, M'nasheh fathered Amon, Amon fathered Yoshiyahu. 11. Yoshiyahu fathered Yochanyahu and his brothers about [the time of] the captivity of Bavel. 12. And after the captivity now of Bavel, Yochanyahu fathered Sh'altiel, Sh'altiel fathered Zerubavel. 13. Zerubavel fathered Awiud, Awiud fathered Elyakim, Elyakim fathered Azor. 14. Azor fathered Tzadoq. Tzadoq fathered Achin, Achin fathered El'ichud. 15. El'ichud fathered El'azar, El'azar fathered Matan, Matan fathered Ya'akov. 16. Ya'akov fathered Yosip, the guardian of Maryam, from whom was born Y'shua, who is called the Mashiyach. 17. Therefore, all the generations from Awraham until Dawid were fourteen generations, and from the captivity of Bavel until the Mashiyach were fourteen generations.

Luke 3:23. And Y'shua was about thirty years old and was to be the son of Yosip, the son of Heli, 24. The son of Mattath the son of Lewi, the son of Malki, the son of Yani, the son of Yosip, 25. The son of Matta, the son of Amos, the son of Nakhum, the son of Khasli, the son of Nagi, the son of Maath, the son of Matath, the son of Shamei, the son of Yosip, the son of Yehuda, 27. the son of Yochanan, the son of Rasa, the son of Zerubavel, the son of Shilathiel, the son of Neri, 28. The son of Malki, the son of Addi, the son of Qusam, the son of Almodad, the son of Ayir, 29. the son of Yoseh, the son of Eliazar, the son of Yoram, the son of Matitha, the son of Lewi, 30. The son of Shimon, the son of Yehuda, the son of Yosip, the son of Yonam, the son of Eliakim, 31. The son of Malia, the son of Manni, the son of Mattha, the son of Nathan, the son of Dawid. 32. The son of Aishi, the son of Obed, the son of Bo'az, the son of Salmon, the son of Nekhshon, 33. The son of Aminadab, the son of Aram, the son of Khetzron, the son of Peretz, the son of Yehuda, 34. The son of Ya'akov, the son of Yitz'chak, the son of Awraham, the son of Terakh, the son of Nakhor 35. The son of Sarug, the son of Araw, the son of Palag, the son of Awar, the son of Shalakh, 36. The son of Qaynan, the son of Arpakshar, the son of Shem, the son of Nukh, the son of Lamakh, 37. The son of Mathushlakh, the son of Knokh, the son of Yared, the son of Mahlalaiel, the son of Qaynan, 38. The son of Anosh, the son of Sheth, the son of Adam, who was from Elohim.

Chapter 1, Question 7: Going by what you've learned so far, what is Torah? What is "legalism"? What do you think "being under the law" means?

Answer: Torah is YAHWEH's "Instructions in Righteousness" - our only guidelines for moral, holy living according to His wishes. Many have mistranslated Torah as the "law" that was supposedly abolished by Jesus – but nothing could be further from the Truth! Legalism consists of the **man-made** concepts which crept into Torah; the traditions and opinions of men. What Yeshua "abolished" was the need to kill an innocent animal for sin sacrifice. He also did His best to show the Pharisees how they had "read into" and twisted YAHWEH's rules to the point where Torah had become a burden.

Chapter 1, Question 8: 1 John 3:4 tells us that sin is?

Answer: Sin is transgression or violation of the Torah. Without Torah mankind would have no way of measuring sin.

Chapter 1, Question 9: Was the Son sent to abolish Torah? Why or why not?

Answer: Absolutely not! The Son did not have the authority to abolish His Father's Divine Instructions! He was sent to *proclaim the Kingdom of* YAHWEH and to do everything the Father told Him:

Luke 4:43. And Y'shua said to them that, It is necessary for me to preach to other cities the Kingdom of Elohim, for because this reason I have been sent.

As a matter of fact, He even spoke of the Kingdom *after* His death!

Acts 1:3. Those who also to whom he revealed himself alive after he had suffered. With numerous signs for forty days he was being seen by them, and he spoke concerning the Kingdom of Elohim.

Chapter 1, Question 10: What, exactly, was "nailed to the cross?"

Answer: Our certificate of debt (Colossians 2:14). This *is not and cannot* be the Torah! These are our sins as measured against man's additions to Torah.

Paul, goes on in his letter: *Colossians 2:15. "And, **by yielding up his body**, he showed contempt for **principalities and authorities**; and **put them to shame**, openly, in his own person. 16. Let no (pagan) therefore judge you about food and drink, or about the distinctions of festivals and new moons and Shabbats 17. which were shadows of the things then future; but the body of Mashiyach. 18. And let no one wish, by abasing the mind, to bring you under bonds that you subject yourselves to the worship of Messengers; 10 while he is prying into that which he has not seen and **is vainly inflated in his fleshly mind** 19. and holds not the head from which the whole body is framed and constructed with joints and members, and grows with the growth (given) of Elohim."*

"Pagan(s)" in verse 16 refers to those non-Jews of the "authorities"; those in verse 15, the "principalities and authorities" who *added* interpretations and restrictions to obedience to Torah! *Yeshua nailed only this to the cross!* Torah is holy and good and instructive; it is the Word of YAHWEH! Yeshua would **never** have "nailed" His own instruction to the cross!

In Colossians 2:18, Paul is saying that, by reducing or lessening that which was made known to you by Messengers (angels-commissioned by YAHWEH) and replacing it with the inflated man-made additions and interpretations, **man's** rule was placed over that of YAHWEH!

No, Torah was not nailed to the cross. Yeshua died to nail to the cross those man-made burdens added to confuse and restrict what was holy and righteous.

Chapter 1, Question 11: In Matthew 5:17 Yeshua said He came not to "loosen but to fulfill" the Torah. What do you think He meant by that?

Answer: As the Word who was with the Father since the beginning (John 1:1-2) He was not sent in the **flesh** to abolish YAHWEH's Divine rules and regulations; He came to "establish/confirm" them. "Fulfill" means to carry out or to bring to realization, to perform or do, as in a person's duty; or to obey or follow the Commandments, as in satisfying the Commandments by obeying them.

Chapter 1, Question 12: Christians insist that "the law" is "written on our hearts" (Jeremiah 31:33-34; Romans 10:4-8) and therefore, the "OT" no longer pertains to them. How can man (who was born into sin) know what "the law" is, if he doesn't first study and learn to obey it?

Answer: Let's view this from another standpoint: Unless we have read and understood the "Old Testament" how can we automatically KNOW what Torah says? Yes, we have "the law"/Torah written on our hearts – however, this does not mean we have an automatic knowledge of it just because we are "saved." It means we now have the **desire** for Torah! We need to remember that the heart is the "seat of desire" as it is the battleground over which YAHWEH and Satan continually fight....

Chapter 1, Question 13: Why would God decide to destroy or change His mind about His own original divine instructions, without which we would have no guide to moral, holy living?

Answer: The answer is clear: He would not. He NEVER changed His mind about holiness or moral behavior, and we are never given any scripture to prove otherwise!

Chapter 1, Question 14: Why are there so many and widely varying Christian denominations (not to mention, world "religions") each claiming to be "the right one"? What was Yeshua's particular "religion" or denomination ?

Answer: There is neither "religion" nor "denomination" in YAHWEH's Kingdom! He is our Creator who gave us rules to follow; yet mankind collectively, came up with their own gods and idols and various religions. Even those who recognized that YAHWEH as THE Creator, kept side-stepping His rules in order to come up with their own ways of worshipping, and that is how Catholicism and Christianity were born. **All** believers are "the seed of Abraham" and therefore, part of Israel (Galatians 3:29), and should therefore be Torah observant believers in Messiah Yeshua.

Chapter 1, Question 15: Why have so many Christian pastors over the years had to step down in shame from their self-indulgent pedestals for one reason or another? Weren't they doing God's will - and if not, why not? How come they were allowed to call themselves "men of the cloth" if they were off doing their own thing?

Answer: No, they were NOT doing God's will! Christians who are under the erroneous assumption that Torah is null and void have **no** guide to holy living. Many, if not most, have clung to the erroneous assumption that "Jesus paid it all" and therefore, they can continue to behave according to the world because they are "forgiven" through the shed blood at the cross. This is a huge mistake, as the Book of Hebrews tells us there is no sin sacrifice for continued, deliberate sinning:

Hebrews 10: 26. For if a man sin voluntarily after he has received a knowledge of the truth, there is no longer a sacrifice which may be offered for sins: 27. but the fearful judgment impends, and the zeal of fire that consumes the adversaries. 28. For if he who transgressed the Torah of Moshe, died without mercies at the mouth of two or three witnesses; 29. how much more, do you think, will he receive capital punishment who has trodden upon the Son of Elohim and has accounted the blood of his covenant by which he is sanctified, as the blood of all men and has treated the Spirit of grace in an insulting manner? 30. For we know him who has said, Retribution is mine and I will repay: and again, Master YHWH will judge his people.

Chapter 1, Question 16: Matthew 5:17-18 says: *Do not think that I have come to loosen Torah or the prophets, I have not come to loosen but to fulfill. For truly I say to you that until heaven and earth pass away not one Yodh or one stroke will pass from Torah until everything happens.* What does "loosen the Torah" mean to you? Has "everything" happened yet? Have heaven and earth passed away?

Answer: No, everything has NOT happened yet, and Yeshua said He did NOT come to "loosen the Torah" or in any way negate Torah. He came to "fulfill" certain prophecies about Himself, but never to "abolish" them….

Chapter 2, Question 1: Please read the following scripture and then write in your own words why YAHWEH would be "tolerant" of "strange/unauthorized fire" (adding to/taking away from His rules) <u>today</u>: *Leviticus 10:1 But Nadav and Avihu, sons of Aaron, each took his censer and after putting fire in it also placed incense inside it and offered strange fire before YHWH, which YHWH had not commanded them to do. Then fire went out from the presence of YHWH and consumed them, and they died before YHWH.*

Answer: The Bible tells us that YAHWEH is the same yesterday, today and forever (Hebrews 13:8), which means He has never changed His mind about "strange fire." The demonstration with Aaron's sons reveals that He is very adamant concerning obedience. The death of Yeshua had nothing, whatsoever, to do with YAHWEH becoming "more tolerant" or loving. He has always loved us; that is why He allowed Adam and Eve to continue living after they sinned. But **love and grace in no way negated** the requirement for obedience. Still today, YAHWEH does not accept "strange fire" – anything added to His *mitzvot*!

Chapter 2, Question 2: Was Torah observance only for "the Jews"? Why or why not?

Answer: No. While YAHWEH originally gave His Torah to the Hebrews (who were ultimately called "Jews," He commanded that ALL who accepted Him as God be Torah observant:

*Numbers 15:13. **All who are native born** will do these things by this method, by presenting an offering by fire as a soothing aroma unto YHWH. 14. **As for the rest in your assembly**, there will be one statute for you and the same statute for the foreigner living with you. 15. This is an **eternal requirement throughout all your generations**, that as you are so shall the foreigner be before YHWH. 16. The same instruction and judgment will apply equally to both you and the foreigner living with you.*

There were no "Jews" until Jacob gave birth to Yehudah (Judah) (Genesis 29:35 and Matthew 1), yet every believer up until then was Torah observant because that is what YAHWEH required....

Chapter 2, Question 3: Exodus 31:13 and Ezekiel 20:12 tells us that the Seventh Day Sabbath is a SIGN between YAHWEH and His people. Where in the Scriptures does YAHWEH tell us to ignore the seventh day Sabbath – the day He Himself blessed and made holy (Genesis 2:1-2)?

Answer: Throughout the Bible one can find absolutely no evidence that YAHWEH or Yeshua ever claimed the first day or placed any special blessing upon it. Furthermore, you won't find anything in the Scriptures that references the changing of the Sabbath to Sunday. Some argue that Constantine was responsible for changing the Sabbath because he hated the Jews. Regardless, in Yeshua's time, both Jews and Gentiles alike attended the synagogues on the seventh day as evidenced in Acts 13:42-44 which shows that the early Gentile believers were Torah observant, in part, because they requested further instruction of Paul "on the next Sabbath" (Saturday/the seventh day). We're told almost the whole city arrived for the meeting on the "next Sabbath" and that no separate Sunday (first day) "sabbaths" were being held by anyone.

Ezekiel 20:11. I gave them My statutes and showed them My ordinances, through which if a person obeys them he will have life through them. 12. I gave them My Shabbats to be a sign between Me and them, so that they would know that I, YHWH, am the One Who makes them Set-Apart.

Isaiah 66:23. From New Moon (month) to New Moon and from Shabbat to Shabbat, all humanity will come and bow down before Me, says YHWH.

Isaiah 58:13. If you turn your foot back from pursuing your own pleasures because of the Shabbat and call the Shabbat a delight and the Set-Apart day of YHWH honorable and then show honor by not going to your own paths or striking bargains, 14. then you can look for the delight of YHWH, and I will set you to ride on the heights of the earth and I will sustain you with the inheritance of your ancestor Ya'akov, for the mouth of YHWH has spoken!

Chapter 2, Question 4: The Catholic "Church Fathers" are responsible for doing away with all things "Jewish" when it comes to the worship of YAHWEH; they are the reason Christians today seem to believe they are exempt from Torah. Can you name some of those "fathers" and how they twisted the Word?

Answer:

- **Ignatius:** He was considered to be an "auditor" and "disciple" of John who pioneered the Greek-based Christian religion and was instrumental in the assimilation of paganism into early Christianity, packaging Christianity for a Greco-Roman Hellenic culture. Ignatius saw Jewish followers of Y'shua as nothing more than legalists and Judaizers. He despised the observance of Shabbat (Sabbath) in favor of his Ishtar (Easter) sunrise "Lord's day" Sun-Day teachings. It is scarcely possible to exaggerate the importance of the Ignatian letters to modern Christian institutions as Ignatius was a key player in the development of the modern Christian church, promoting the "infallibility of the church" and the "universal church" which had incorporated large doses of paganism. If there ever was a hierarchy loving "Christian" with a Hellenistic autocratic mindset, it was Ignatius who gave himself the nickname Theophoros (the God-bearer) and taught that deacons, presbyters and bishops were a separate category of people, high and lifted up, and infused with Jesus-like authority to be lords over people. Christians consider Ignatius as one of the all time biggest movers and shakers of the all-Gentile church. He strongly instructed that "without the bishop's supervision, no baptisms or love feasts are permitted." He also believed Mary to be the eternal virgin mother of God.

- **Tertullian:** One of Tertullian's better known "achievements" was to fall into a trance and then prophesy under the influence of the "Holy Spirit" insisting his utterances were the voice of the "Holy Spirit." While fumbling in all manner of paganism and spiritism, Tertullian picked up an "anointing" of the "Holy Ghost" and coined the word "Trinity" which is one of the most beloved doctrines of the Church to this very day (more on this in a later chapter). The "persons of the trinity" doctrine flourishes in the hierarchy-based religion which sees itself as a three-sided pyramid structure. Tertullian's works abound with puns, wit, sarcasm and a continual pounding of his opponents with invectives.

- **Marcion:** Every Christian who uses the term "Old" and "New" testament must take their hats off to Marcion as he was the one who coined these terms which perfectly reflect the Hellenistic mindset of the pagan world which is ignorant of Torah. Marcion taught that the Old and New Testaments could not be reconciled with each other, and this is what we hear in Christian churches today.

Chapter 2, Question 5:   Many Catholic and Christian churches feature "Jesus hanging on a cross." In your opinion, is this right or wrong?

Answer: *So pay great and careful attention! Since you did not see any form whatsoever on the day that YHWH your Elohim spoke to you at Horeb from the midst of the fire, that you do not act in a destructive and perverse way and make for yourselves and make a graven image for yourself in the form of any figure, the likeness of a male or a female... (Deuteronomy 4:15-16)*

Let's be realistic: The beloved "cross" that Catholics and Christians like to hang around their necks and place in their homes and churches is actually a ***symbol of a pagan Roman death device with a dead man hanging on it***! Is that what YAHWEH is all about - dying in agony and being perceived by the world as "dead"? Can GOD die? Can GOD be born? Did GOD have a "mother" as the Catholics insist?

No, but His SON did; the **Man** who walked this earth for a brief time to proclaim the Kingdom and show us how to properly worship and behave according to the commands of His Father.

But his is exactly the type of thing Satan wants you to focus on! He wants you to get the subliminal message that "God" is dead. Our Savior – YAHWEH's Son, a man who was able to do nothing until after He was baptized (John 8:40, Acts 10:37-38)) - hung on a stake for approximately **six hours and was removed** because the Judeans wanted Him off the cross and in the grave before sundown so as not to desecrate the holy day of Passover.

John 19:14. And it was the eve of the Paskha (Passover), and it was about the sixth hour, and he said to the Yehudeans, "Behold your King!"

John 19:31. And the Yehudeans, because it was the eve, said, "These bodies should not remain on their stakes because the Shabbat is dawning." For it was a high day, the day of the Shabbat, that they entreated from Peelatos (Pilate) that they might break the legs of those who were nailed to the stake and take them down.

Yeshua was **removed** from that hideous pagan death device, yet Christians keep on leaving "Jesus" hanging there day in and day out. For the last two thousand years they've been concentrating on those six agonizing hours instead of the overall picture, which is His gift of **eternal life**. How is that glorifying YAHWEH or Yeshua?

Yeshua's death – while very important because it was necessary for us to gain eternal life – does **not** represent the whole picture of God and His Torah - yet Christians keep on crucifying "Jesus" *ad nauseum.* They just cannot let Him come down off that cross!

Yes, His death mattered! He had to die to become our Final Sin Sacrifice! But there's more: HE ROSE; He overcame death and the "world" (Matthew 28) and He is returning (Revelation 11:15) to rule and reign a thousand years until Judgment Day when YAHWEH will give us a "new heaven and a new earth" (Revelation 21). **That** is what we are to focus on! He was the Word of YAHWEH in the flesh who came to preach the Kingdom of YAHWEH (Luke 4:43) and to show us how to properly obey His Father as He himself also did. In the meantime, our job is to get to know YAHWEH and His Son by nurturing a relationship based on obedience!

Chapter 2, Question 6:   Numbers 15:13-16 shows YAHWEH reiterating four times that everyone who accepts Him is to do exactly as His Torah observant people do and that this is to be done "throughout your generations."   As a grafted-in believer in Yeshua (Romans 11:16-18), do you believe this includes you? Why or why not?

Answer: Every believing Gentile needs to know that they are part of Israel because they have been grafted in through the atoning blood of Messiah Yeshua! As such, they must do exactly as the "natural branches" – which means, they must be Torah observant. Same God, same rules!

Romans 11:16. For, if the first-fruits (are) Set Apart, then the rest of the dough (it came from is) also: and if the root is Set Apart, then also the branches. 17. And if some of the branches were plucked off; and you, an olive from the desert, were in-grafted in their place and have become an heir of the root and fatness of the olive-tree; 18. Do not boast over the branches. For if you boast, you do not sustain the root, but the root sustains you. 19. And should you say the branches were plucked off that I might be grafted into their place. 20. Very true. They were plucked off because they disbelieved; and you stand by faith. But do not be uplifted in your mind, but fear. 21. For if Elohim spared not the natural branches, perhaps he will not spare you. 22. Behold now the goodness and the severity of Elohim: on them who fell, severity; but on you, goodness, if you continue in that goodness; and if not, you also will be plucked off. 23. And they, if they do not continue in their poverty of faith, even they will be grafted in; for Elohim is able to graft them in again. 24. For if you were plucked from the wild olive-tree which was natural to you, and were grafted, contrary to your nature, into a good olive-tree; how much more may they be grafted into their natural olive-tree.

Chapter 2, Question 7: With whom did YAHWEH make His New Covenant?

Answer: Not with the Gentiles or with any particular "religion" but with the Torah observant houses of Israel and Judah!

Jeremiah 31:31. Behold! The day is coming, says YHWH, when I will carve out a new covenant with the house of Israel and the house of Yehudah. 32. It will not be like the covenant I made with their ancestors in the day when I took them by the hand and brought them out of the land of Egypt, because the broke My covenant even though I was a husband to them, says YHWH. 33. But this is the covenant I will carve out with the house of Israel after those days. Proclaims YHWH: I will put My Torah-instruction deep within them and within their innermost being will I write it. And I will be their Elohim and they shall be My people. 34. No longer will everyone teach their neighbor to know YHWH for they will all know Me, from the least of them to the greatest of them. (And) YHWH has spoken: 35. For I will forgive their depravity and remember their sin no more. 36. And YHWH also says: Who gives the sun for a light by day and the ordinances of the moon and of the stars as a light for the night? Who divides and stirs up the sea into thunderous waves? YHWH Tsavaot {of Hosts} is His Name!

Romans 10:12. And in this, it discriminates neither Jews nor Gentiles. For there is one, Master YHWH, over them all, who is abundantly generous towards every one that calls on him. 13. For everyone that will call on the name of Master YHWH, will have life.

Remember, the House of Israel includes ALL believers in Messiah Yeshua, which includes YOU - Halleluyah!

Chapter 2, Question 8: What is meant by "Hebrew mindset" vs. "Greek mindset"?

Answer: It refers to the idea that there is a discrepancy between the Jewish and Christian concepts about life, God and Truth; in other words, they were "set" in their respective ways of thinking about these issues. In the mindset of the Hebrews, **YAHWEH** was the Creator. Period. Greeks, on the other hand, were Gentiles prone to be atheistic, agnostic, or into pagan gods – and that's why the Apostle Paul used different methods when he spoke to the Hebrew and Greek cultures.

Example: The "Greek" mindset visualizes a tattoo (or something similar) on the thigh of Jesus when he returns as "King of Kings, and Lord of Lords" (Revelation 19:11-13, 16), while the Hebrew mindset sees something deeper, more realistic, more Torah-based. The Hebrew mindset visualizes Yeshua, the Torah observant Jewish Messiah wrapped in a *tallit* (prayer shawl) as He sits atop a white horse, headed back to Earth with the *tzitzits* (braids, knots, tassels) that fall across His thighs spelling out the Name of YAHWEH. (Each letter of the Hebrew alphabet has a numerical value and, consequently, the number of knots on the tzit-tzits on the four corners of a tallit, tied properly, spell out the name of YAHWEH. No tattoo required!)

Another example of a Hebrew as opposed to Greek mindset can be seen in the respective calendars/timelines. YAHWEH's timelines are amply evidenced throughout the Bible, whereas our Gregorian calendars are speckled with the names of pagan deities representing the days and months. According to YAHWEH, a "day" is **not** from midnight to midnight, but from "sunset to sunset" (Genesis 1:5). He called the days of the week the "first day," "second day," etc., whereas "the world" has named its days and months after pagan gods and goddesses.

Chapter 2, Question 9: Please read Luke 4. How did Yeshua respond to Satan's questions and comments when he tried to tempt Yeshua? From where did His quotes originate?

Answer: He answered "It is written...." What was written? The *Tanakh* ("Old" Testament)! He didn't try to argue with the enemy; He simply quoted what was written in the Scriptures – the part of the Bible that contained the very words of YAHWEH Himself which often ended with, "Thus saith the Lord!"

Chapter 2, Question 10: When, according to the Bible, was Yeshua born and where in the Bible are we told to celebrate His birth??

Answer: According to the Bible, Yeshua was born on the first day of Sukkot/Feast of Tabernacles (which falls in the September/October timeframe on our Gregorian calendars) and He was circumcised on the eighth day according to YAHWEH's command (Genesis 17:12). Nowhere in the Scriptures are we ever told to celebrate the birth of Yeshua; although, in all fairness, we aren't told NOT to, either.

We can know the time of His birth by closely studying the Hebrew calendar, the timing of the Feasts and the "tours of duty" for the priests which, in John the Baptist's case was important because his father Zachariah was a priest who impregnated his wife Elisheva (Elizabeth) late in the third month, Sivan (Luke 1:23-24).

According to Luke, Chapter 1, Yeshua was conceived by the Holy Spirit in the sixth month of Elisheva's (Elisabeth's) pregnancy. This study could fill another book, in itself, but the short version is, Luke Chapter 2 explains that when Miriam and Yosef came to Bethlehem they could find no room at the inn. Why? Because Miriyam's husband Yosef was from Galilee, the pair was forced to go to Jerusalem for the census that year. Unfortunately, since all the men of Israel had come to attend the eight-day celebration of the Feast of Sukkot (Tabernacles), every room for miles around Jerusalem (which is approximately 5 miles from Bethlehem) had already been taken. Therefore, the only place available when Miriam went into labor was a stable.

Luke 2:1. Now it happened in those days that a decree went out from Augustus Caesar that the names of all the people of his dominion should be written down.

Luke 2:6. And it happened that while they were there, her days of pregnancy were fulfilled. 7. And she bore him a firstborn son and wrapped him in swaddling clothes, and laid him in a manger because there was no room where they could lodge.

Luke 2:8. At this time shepherds were there in that region were they were lodging and keeping watch there at night over their flocks. 9. And behold a Messenger of Elohim came to them. And the glory of Master YHWH shone upon them and they feared with a great fear! 10. And the Messenger said to them, "Do not have fear, for behold I announce hope to you! A great joy which will be to the whole world. 11. For today is born to you in the city of Dawid the Savior who is Master YHWH, the Mashiyach. 12. And this is a sign to you; you will find an infant who is wrapped in swaddling clothes and lying in a manger."

NOTE: Luke 2:11 contains one of the most powerful statements about YAHWEH and His Mashiyach! YAHWEH is the real Mashiyach, who chose the vessel of Yeshua the man. However, within Yeshua the man is an occurrence of the One Divine Nature of YAHWEH, also known as the *Ruach haKodesh*. This is the literal meaning of the fullness of YAHWEH dwelling inside Mashiyach, and in accordance with *Tanakh* prophecy (Isaiah 53:1, Zechariah 12:10). The divine and human natures exist separately yet side-by-side within Yeshua.

Luke 2:21. Then when eight days had passed so that the boy could be circumcised, they called his name Y'shua, as the Messenger had called him before he was conceived in the womb. 22. And when the days of their purification were fulfilled according to the instruction of Moshe, they took him up to Urishlim to present him before Master YHWH, 23. According to what is written in the Torah of Master YHWH that every male who opens the womb will be called a Set Apart one of Master YHWH.

Despite the fact that Yeshua was born in the September/October timeframe many Christians insist on celebrating the man-made "holiday" of Christmas on December 25th, justifying this with comments such as, "Who cares when Jesus was born - **we** celebrate His birth in December!"

The truth is, YAHWEH arranged for His Son to be born in His timing - as revealed in His *Mo'edim* - Biblical Feasts/Appointed Times, all of which foreshadow Yeshua who has so far fulfilled on the first FOUR of the SEVEN Feasts - and there are just three more to go!

One of the Feasts Yeshua fulfilled, of course, was His own birthday.

If you are still among those who insist that the lie of "Christmas" doesn't matter, then please consider the following (from Andrew Gabriel Roth) which supports the fact that "Jesus" was NOT born in December, which makes "Christmas" a complete lie:

• Shepherds do not "abide in the fields" in December with their sheep in Israel, not 2,000 years ago and not now. It is well known that shepherds stay in shelters starting in November, with the arrival of the rainy season.

• If you know what the Star of Bethlehem is (Jupiter) then you know when the Nativity was. The Magi told Herod "the time the star appeared" and Herod killed infants two years and under in response. That means the Magi were tracking the "king's star" for two years, because Herod didn't stop from killing his own children and his favorite wife, per Josephus. In fact, Josephus says that Augustus Caesar himself remarked that he would rather be one of Herod's dogs than one of his children. The only "star of kings" that Magi would have known was Jupiter. "Magi" refers to Zoroastrian priests from either Babylon or Persia (Iran or Iraq), both of which are EAST of Israel and both tracked a triple conjunction of Jupiter (the king's planet) and Saturn (the savior planet for the Jews) in Aries (the zodiac sing for Syria and Israel in their mythology). Zoroastrians had a myth that their version of

Messiah, called "Saoshyant" in their scriptures, would be born "in the west, in a foreign land." When the triple conjunction, along with a comet and other things, all began in 7 BCE, they knew they had to grab the incense and go. Jupiter even went behind the sun and "died" - was invisible, for more than a year. It emerged triumphantly from behind the sun in mid 6 BCE and tracked west for 4 months, pausing over Bethlehem on Sept. 5 BCE.

• As if that isn't compelling enough, remember Luke tells us Zechariah, John the Baptist's father, served 15 months in the Temple before Messiah was born. Luke gives us the name of the course: Abijah (Luke 1:5). Guess what? We know when Abijah served during this time, and when we add 15 months it comes again to Sept, 5 BCE.

• Likewise we can date the first census of Qurinius as well, as Romans counted folks every 14 years and people in Egypt - like Josef and Mary - were forced to return to their ANCESTRAL HOMES to pay the tax. This is verified in the Bible; it is not open to interpretation!

• Luke and John synch on the same year for the beginning of Messiah's ministry: 27 BCE. How do we know that? Forty-six years from the beginning of Herod's temple and the 15th year of Tiberius bring us to the same year. Co-regencies were counted as part of Roman rule, so Tiberius co-ruled with Augustus starting in 12 CE. Josephus says Herod began building the Temple in 19 BCE. Then Luke says Y'shua was "about 30" when he began his ministry. By this clock, he would be 30 years exactly and a few months. (No year 0 in the timeline so 4 years to 1 BCE +26 to get to Rosh Hashana = 30).

Chapter 2, Question 11: From your own understanding of the Bible, can **God** be born to a human being, wear diapers, be "a *man* of pains, well acquainted with illness" (Isaiah 53:3) or die? Why, or why not??

Answer: Absolutely not! God has always been and always will be. He has no mother or father.

Genesis 1:1. In the beginning YHWH created the heavens and the earth.

Exodus 3:13. Moshe said to Elohim, "Look, when I appear before the people of Isra'el and say to them, 'The Elohim of your ancestors has sent me to you'; and they ask me, 'What is his name?'

what am I to tell them?" 14. Elohim said to Moshe, "Ehyeh Asher Ehyeh [I am Who I am, I will be What I am]," and added, "Here is what to say to the people of Isra'el: 'Ehyeh [I Am or I Will Be] has sent me to you.'" 15. **Elohim said then to Moshe, "Say this to the people of Isra'el: 'YAHWEH [He is], the Elohim of your fathers, the Elohim of Avraham, the Elohim of Yitz'chak and the Elohim of Ya'akov, has sent me to you.' This is my name for all time; this is how generation after generation is to remember Me."**

John 1:*1. In the beginning was the Miltha* ('Word', 'Manifestation', 'Instance' or 'Substance' among other things). *And that Miltha was with Elohim. And Elohim was that Miltha. 2. This was with Elohim in the beginning. 3. Everything existed through His hands, and without Him, not even one thing existed of the things which have existed. 4. In Him was life, and the life was the light of men. 5. And that light shines in the darkness, and the darkness did not overtake it.*

Chapter 2, Question 12: Since God cannot be born or die, how is it that "Jesus" is God, and when and where was He ever given the authority to abolish His Father's Divine Instructions to mankind (Torah)?

Answer: (This question was designed to make you think about the relationship between Yeshua and His Father. Yeshua was definitely the Word of YAHWEH come in the flesh, but remember, He did *not* come to replace YAHWEH....) Yeshua was "the Word" (John 1:1) who, we are told, has been around since the beginning. He was sent to earth by YAHWEH as a human with a Divine qnoma (nature) to teach mankind about God and how to worship Him, and then to martyr Himself as the Final SIN Sacrifice. Yeshua said He came NOT to abolish but to fulfill (Matthew 5:17) the prophecies and to proclaim the Kingdom of Yahweh (Luke 4:43).

Chapter 3, Question 1: The Bible in several places states that Yahweh's Word is forever. Can you explain why Yeshua's death on the stake would suddenly abolish Yahweh's original Divine instructions or negate His "forever" commands? Did "forever" end at the beginning of the "New Testament"?

Answer: No! Forever never ends. YAHWEH said His Torah would stand forever (2 Chronicles 7:14-22), and many of His "forever" commands will end up in eternity with us:

- The Seventh Day Sabbath (Exodus 31:13-17; Leviticus 23:3) is a "forever" be a sign between Him and the children of Israel (which includes every believer, grafted-in or otherwise!) In the end times (which we are in now) the seventh day Sabbath will distinguish TRUE believers from the "lukewarm" - especially when the Antichrist starts putting pressure on people to conform to his rules.

  *Exodus 31:12. And YHWH spoke to Moshe saying, 13. "Speak to the people of Israel and say, 'You will surely keep watch and account of my Shabbats, for this is a sign between Me and you **throughout all your generations**, so that you will know that I am YHWH who has set you apart for Me. 14. Therefore you are to keep my Shabbat (seventh day weekly) because it is set-apart for you. Everyone who treats it as if it were a regular day must be put to death; for whoever does any work on it is to be cut away from the inward parts of his people. ... 16. So the people of Israel are keep watch over and preserve the Shabbat, to **maintain the Shabbat throughout all their generations as a perpetual covenant**. 17. It is a sign between Me and the people of Israel for all eternity, for in six days YHWH made the heavens and the earth, but on the seventh day He completed His work and rested.'"*

- The Biblical feasts are outlined in Leviticus 23. Each feast outline includes a statement something to the effect of: "This is a permanent regulation throughout all your generations," or "It shall be a statute for ever in all your dwellings throughout your generations."

- Keeping kosher. Yes, eating "clean" foods was a "forever" command. The "garbage disposal" animals (birds, fish, animals that eat other dead animals) were NOT "made clean" when Yeshua died! They are still "garbage disposals" prone to carry diseases. For a complete outline, see Deuteronomy 14:1-21 and Leviticus 11.

The above is by no means a complete list, but it will give you a good start and a lot to think about.

Psalm 119:89. "Forever, O YHWH, is Your Word established in Heaven!."

*Isaiah 59:21. –As for Me, **this is My covenant with them: My Spirit which is upon you and My Words which I have set in your mouth will never depart from your mouth or from the mouths of your children or from the mouths of their children, says YHWH! So it will be forever.***

"Forever" hasn't come unless "everything has happened that must happen" and "heaven and earth have passed away" (Revelation 21:1). Has the heavenly Jerusalem already come down from heaven to the Earth (Revelation 21:2)? Has Satan already been punished and cast into the lake of fire? (Revelation 20:10.) Has the Great White Throne Judgment occurred already? (Revelation 20:11-12.) Has Yeshua already returned and established the Kingdom of God (Revelation 10:1-7 and 19:6, 11-16)? (Also see Isaiah 59:21 and 1 Chronicles 16:15.)

Since Yeshua said He did NOT come to abolish Torah, we MUST adhere to Torah! The Bible clearly shows that Yeshua was a Jew who did not come to abolish the faith of Judaism or the Torah, but to magnify, establish, and confirm it. And He said:

Matthew 5:19. All who loosen, therefore, from one (of) these small commandments and teach thus to the sons of man, will be called little in the Kingdom of Heaven, but all who do and teach this will be called great in the Kingdom of Heaven. 20. For I say to you that unless your righteousness exceeds more than that of the scribes and the Pharisees, you will not enter the Kingdom of Heaven.

Chapter 3, Question 2: Can you find any evidence anywhere in the Bible where YAHWEH ever dropped His Standards for Torah, just because the human race was disobedient? If so, please write the pertinent scripture references here:

Answer: YAHWEH is the same today, yesterday and forever (Hebrews 13:8). Man's philosophies, customs, traditions, mores, values, knowledge, societies and even his language continuously grows, "morphs" or changes, but YAHWEH's Standards for Righteousness do not. Regardless as to what level of progress our society is undergoing at any given time, YAHWEH always expects us to lead holy lives.

Chapter 3, Question 3: YAHWEH has endless patience with those who are trying their best to obey His Commands, but He removes His Hand and His Grace from those who refuse to follow Him (as was the case with Pharaoh). Still, many are quick to point out that we no longer have to bother with Torah because we are no longer under the law but, rather, under grace. When and where in the Bible do you think "grace" began, and did it give us permission to ignore God's rules??

Answer: Contrary to popular opinion, "grace" did not first crop up with the death of Yeshua. "Grace" began with Adam and Eve in the Garden of Eden when, instead of wiping the pair from the face of the earth, YAHWEH killed an innocent animal to atone for their sins, and then put them into "the world" where they could experience firsthand the "knowledge of good and evil"....

Grace continued into the life of Cain after he killed Abel. Grace continued into Noah's time when Noah and his family were the only ones saved from the Flood. Grace continued when YAHWEH gave us His awesome Son who chose to die on our behalf! And grace continues through today, despite the fact that the world is now experiencing the same satanic decadence that had saturated the core of humanity "in the days of Noah."

Grace will continue into the Millennium, after YAHWEH's holy, Torah observant believers have been "raptured" and help Yeshua rule and reign the earth for a thousand years. Grace will allow those who wish to follow Satan into hell, to do so:

Revelation 20:7. And when these thousand years will be completed, Satan will be released from his prison; 8. and will go forth to seduce the nations that are in the four corners of the earth, Gog and Magog; and to assemble them for battle, whose number is as the sand of the sea. 9. And they went up on the breadth of the earth and encompassed the camp of the Set Apart believers and the beloved city. And fire came down from Elohim out of heaven and consumed them. 10. And the Accuser who seduced them, was cast into the lake of fire and sulfur, where also were the beast of prey and the false prophet: and they will be tormented, day and night, forever and ever.

Isaiah 14:15 states that Satan will be brought down to hell and a slaughter is prepared for his children (verse 21). Rev 20:10 promises a date for Satan in the lake of fire, in the meantime we are to recognize that our battles are not against flesh and blood, and to act accordingly. That is GRACE because YAHWEH allows mankind free will until the very end.

Grace and mercy have **never** invalidated Torah!

Chapter 3, Question 4: John 17:3 informs us that eternal life is knowing God and knowing Yeshua. Is there any way outside of Torah that we can possibly "know God." If so, how?

Answer: No! YAHWEH is the Creator who gave us His holy Torah without which we would have no blueprint for moral, holy living.

Chapter 3, Question 5: According to Jeremiah 31:30-32, with whom did YAHWEH make His "new covenant" and how does if affect you?

Answer: He made His New Covenant with the Torah observant houses of Israel (which also includes those Gentiles who accept YAHWEH) and Judah. Numbers 15:13-16 tell us four times that He expects ALL to obey His Torah, and this was never negated by the Apostle Paul or anyone else. Yeshua personally showed us how to "walk the walk" and then died to offer YAHWEH's people the chance for eternal life and to be a beacon of light for Him via their actions until the day they pass away into eternity.

Chapter 3, Question 6: John 10:30 says: *I and the Father are one.* Hebrews 13:8 tells us YAHWEH is the same yesterday, today and forever. So, why would He have sent His Son?

Answer: The answer is simple: Yeshua showed us how to do it; we are to follow in His footsteps and obey, which is scattered throughout the Gospels:

Matthew 16:24. Then Y'shua said to his disciples, **He who wishes to follow after me, let him deny himself and take up his staff and follow after me.** *25. He who desires to save his life, will lose it. And he who loses his life for my sake, will find it. 26. For what does it profit a man if he gains all the world, and loses his soul? Or what will a man give in exchange for his soul? 27. For it is necessary for the Son of man to come in the glory of his Father.* **And then with his Set Apart Messengers he will reward each man according to his work.**

Chapter 3, Question 7: When did YAHWEH ever indicate that Torah would be "nailed to the cross" or that it was to be considered a "curse" after Yeshua's death, as most Christians today insist?

Answer: Many attempt to use the misunderstood writings of Paul who said:

Colossians 2:14. and, by his mandates, he blotted out the handwriting of our debts which (handwriting) existed against us, and took (it) from the midst and affixed (it) to his stake.

195

Viewed in context, you can see that Paul was trying to explain that Yeshua wiped away the documented opinions of men (bill of charges/handwriting of our debts) against us and took them from our midst. He never said a thing about Torah being "nailed to the cross!"

The Torah is holy, righteous and good (Romans 7:12). To suddenly have it "nailed to the cross" would mean that the things of God were originally evil, something to be done away with. Rav Sha'ul also said, concerning the opinions of men:

Colossians 2:16. Let no (pagan) therefore judge you about food and drink, or about the distinctions of festivals and new moons and Shabbats 17. which were shadows of the things then future....

This doesn't mean Rav Sha'ul was negating Torah. He was warning about the opinions of men concerning these things - **not** giving permission to transgress or dismiss them.

Chapter 3, Question 8: As grafted in believers, Gentiles are part of Israel, and as such, do you believe YAHWEH would treat His "adopted children" any differently from His "natural" ones? Why or why not?

Answer: No, He would not. Same God, same rules – exactly as outlined in Numbers 15:13-16.

Chapter 3, Question 9: Who are "the people of Isra'el"?

Answer: Everyone who accepts the God of Abraham, Isaac and Jacob.

Romans 10:12. And in this, it discriminates neither Jews nor Gentiles. For there is one, Master YHWH, over them all, who is abundantly generous towards every one that calls on him. 13. For everyone that will call on the name of Master YHWH, will have life.

Romans 11:16. For, if the first-fruits (are) Set Apart, then the rest of the dough (it came from is) also: and if the root is Set Apart, then also the branches. 17. And if some of the branches were plucked off; and you, an olive from the desert, were in-grafted in their place and have become an heir of the root and fatness of the olive-tree; 18. Do not boast over the branches. For if you boast, you do not sustain the root, but the root sustains you. 19. And should you say the branches were plucked off that I might be grafted into their place. 20. Very true. They were plucked off because they disbelieved; and you stand by faith. But do not be uplifted in your mind, but fear. 21. For if Elohim spared not the natural branches, perhaps he will not spare you. 22. Behold now the goodness and the severity of Elohim: on them who fell, severity; but on you, goodness, if you continue in that goodness; and if not, you also will be plucked off. 23. And they, if they do not continue in their poverty of faith, even they will be grafted in; for Elohim is able to graft them in again. 24. For if you were plucked from the wild olive-tree which was natural to you, and were grafted, contrary to your nature, into a good olive-tree; how much more may they be grafted into their natural olive-tree? 25. (For I want you to know this) mystery, that blindness of heart has in some measure befallen Israel until the fullness of the Gentiles will come in: 26. And then will all Israel live.

Chapter 3, Question 10: Please study the following scriptures and explain who the people are who obey God's commands AND bear witness to Yeshua:

*Revelation 12:17. And the dragon was enraged against the woman; and he went to make war upon the remnant of her seed who keep the Commandments of Elohim **and** have the testimony of Y'shua.*

*Revelation 14:12. Here is the patience of the Set Apart believers who keep the commandments of Elohim, **and** the faith of Y'shua.*

Answer: Torah observant believers in Messiah Yeshua!

Chapter 3, Question 11: In Revelation 12:17, at whom is the Dragon enraged?

Answer: Those who hold to the Testimony of Yeshua, AND obey His Commandments!

Chapter 3, Question 12: What does it mean to OBEY God? What, exactly, are you as a Christian, obeying?

Answer: Obeying God means paying attention to all the rules we possibly can, especially the rules to keep the Seventh Day Sabbath and the Biblical Feasts, and eating only kosher foods. As believers Christians are actually already obeying some rules (i.e., the Ten Commandments) but by ignoring the true Sabbath and the Feasts while munching on a Christmas ham, they are guilty of gross disobedience....

Chapter 3, Question 13: Throughout the Bible we can see that YAHWEH's covenants, although modified according to His will, were never negated, abolished or replaced. What, exactly, changed when we received the "New Covenant"?

Answer:

(1) Yeshua, as the word of YAHWEH in the flesh (not "incarnate" because that denotes God died!), is now the standard bearer. Moses is no longer the steward, thereby fulfilling the prophecy of Deuteronomy 18:18.

(2) The Torah is administered (not replaced) under a new covenant – It is now written on our hearts via the Spirit of YAHWEH, and not on clay tablets alone, thus fulfilling the prophecy of **Jeremiah 31:31-33.**

(3) The priesthood has changed. Instead of an Aharonic high priest, the high priest is Yeshua – fulfilling the prophecy of Psalm 110:1-4.

(4) The sacrificial system has changed. Under the original covenant, animal sacrifices were offered. Under the new covenant, Messiah Himself is the sacrifice. This fulfills the foreshadowing of Psalms 40:6-7.

Chapter 3, Question 14: YAHWEH considers His Seventh Day Sabbath a SIGN between Him and His people (Exodus 31:16-17). That being the case, please find the scripture that tells us where His Sabbath (day of rest) was changed to the "first day."

Answer: There isn't one! Christianity insists the Sabbath changed to the first "when Jesus died," but this is totally unsubstantiated by the fact that Yeshua was our final SIN Sacrifice, not someone who came to alter His Father's Divine Rules.

Chapter 4, Question 1: When were the first known Torah commands originally given?

Answer: In the Garden of Eden when YAHWEH told Adam and Eve to refrain from eating of the tree of the knowledge of good and evil (Genesis 2:16-17). He continued adding more rules as the population grew, and they culminated in the giving of the Ten Commandments on Mt. Sinai (Exodus 24:3-7).

Chapter 4, Question 2: What does the forgiveness of sin require?

Answer: The shedding of the blood of an innocent animal. (Leviticus 4:27; 6:17-20; etc.)

Chapter 4, Question 3: When was the first known sin sacrifice performed?

Answer: The first known sacrifice was when YAHWEH killed an animal in the Garden of Eden to cover the sin of Adam and Eve (Genesis 3:21).

Chapter 4, Question 4: When did the last known sin sacrifice occur?

Answer: On the day Yeshua was nailed to the stake. (See the Gospels of Matthew, Mark, Luke and John.)

Chapter 4, Question 5: What is the ultimate consequence of sin?

Answer: Death, eternal separation from YAHWEH. (Romans 6:23)

Chapter 4, Question 6: When did YAHWEH start doling out "grace" and who were the recipients?

Answer: When He allowed Adam and Eve to live outside the Garden after they broke the command not to eat from the tree of the knowledge of good and evil (Genesis 2:16-17).

Chapter 4, Question 7: How do we know Cain and Abel were Torah observant?

Answer: They offered sacrifices to YAHWEH (Genesis 4:3-4).

Chapter 4, Question 8: How do we know Noah was Torah observant?

Answer: Because he knew the difference between "clean" and "unclean" animals (Genesis 7:2-15).

Chapter 4, Question 9: Were any of the following "Jews"? Adam, Eve, Cain, Abel, Noah? (Think about how many generations passed [Abraham, Isaac and Jacob!] before "Jews" came onto the scene – and yet every believer up until then was already Torah observant!)

Answer: There were no "Jews" until Jacob gave birth to Judah (Genesis 29:35 and Matthew 1), where the term "Jew" eventually originated.

Chapter 4, Question 10: Genesis 7:2-15 tell us that Noah was commanded to take both "clean" and "unclean" animals onto the ark with him. In your own words, why do you suppose that was?

Answer: YAHWEH had decreed some animals (the "garbage disposals" that eat other dead animal carcasses, etc.) to be "unclean" and unfit for human consumption. These animals would be needed in the post-flood world in order to continue the environmental synergy and balance, but they were never intended as food for humans, as those who belong to YAHWEH are to be clean in body, mind, spirit, thought and deed (Deuteronomy 6:4-5; I Corinthians 10:31; I Corinthians 6:19, etc.)

Chapter 4, Question 11: Exodus 12:38 tells us Isra'el consisted of "a mixed crowd" accompanying Moshe out of Egypt. Exodus 19:8 and 24:3 show that Isra'el accepted YAHWEH's offer to obey His "every word." What is the significance of these statements?

Answer: This shows that Isra'el includes not only the Hebrews/Jews but anyone who accepts the God of Abraham, Isaac and Jacob (Exodus 12:49 and Numbers 9:14) who is the "same yesterday, today and forever" (Hebrews 13:8). One God, one set of rules! We're all equal in His eyes.)

Chapter 4, Question 12: Many who sin are quick to cry, "You're judging me!" when someone attempts to tell them to stop sinning. The Bible, however, commands us to correct sinners (Titus 1:13, 2 Tim. 2:15, etc.), and James 2:12 tells us that _____, not man's opinions, are one's judge. It is NOT "judging" when we weigh someone's actions against what _____ says.

Answer: Both answers are Torah!

Chapter 4, Question 13: If the Torah was "abolished" and the "Old Testament" doesn't pertain to today's believers, why are Christian pastors still teaching the Ten Commandments or telling church members to tithe?

Answer: Because they don't know the Scriptures in their proper context, yet are picking and choosing which ones will benefit them – simple as that!

Chapter 4, Question 14: Was Torah just for "the Jews"? Why or why not?

Answer: No. Numbers 15:13-16 explains in detail that **anyone** who accepts YAHWEH must be Torah observant.

Chapter 4, Question 15: What conditions changed when YAHWEH made a "new covenant" with the Houses of Israel and Judah?

Answer:

(1) The Steward: Yeshua, as the word of YAHWEH in the flesh (not "incarnate" because that denotes God died!), is now the standard bearer. Moses is no longer the steward, thereby fulfilling the prophecy of **Deuteronomy 18:***18. I will raise up for them a prophet like you from among their kinsmen. I will put my words in his mouth, and he will tell* *them everything I order him. 19. Whoever doesn't listen to my words, which he will speak in my name, will have to account for himself to me.*

(2) The Torah is administered (not replaced) under a new covenant – It is now written on our hearts via the Spirit of YAHWEH, and not on clay tablets alone, thus fulfilling the prophecy of **Jeremiah 31:***31. Behold! The day is coming, says YHWH, when I will carve out a new covenant with the house of Israel and the house of Yehudah. 32. It will not be like the covenant I made with their ancestors in the day when I took them by the hand and brought them out of the land of Egypt, because the broke My covenant even though I was a husband to them, says YHWH. 33. But this is the covenant I will carve out with the house of Israel after those days. Proclaims YHWH: I will put My Torah-instruction deep within them and within their innermost being will I write it. And I will be their Elohim and they shall be My people. 34. No longer will everyone teach their neighbor to know YHWH for they will all know Me, from the least of them to the greatest of them. (And) YHWH has spoken: 35. For I will forgive their depravity and remember their sin no more.*

Again, please note that YAHWEH made His "New Covenant" **not** with the Gentiles, or the Christians or the Muslims or anyone except for the Houses of Israel and Judah.

Also, please note that many who believe "Torah is now written on our hearts" are under the erroneous assumption that they don't have to do anything but "believe in Jesus."   What this actually means, however, is that we are willing to follow YAHWEH's instruction and learn and obey Torah; NOT that we are born with an innate knowledge about His teachings and commands which we can ignore at will!

(3) The priesthood has changed. Instead of an Aharonic high priest, the high priest is Yeshua – fulfilling the prophecy of Psalms 110, where King David writes: *1. YHWH says to my human master. Sit at My right hand, until I set your enemies before you like a footstool for your feet. 2. YHWH will stretch your mighty scepter from Zion saying: Have dominion in the midst of all your enemies. Your people will come forward willingly 3. on that day of Your power, in Set-Apart splendor, from the womb of the dawn! Yours was the dew of youth. 4. YHWH has sworn it and He will never go back on His Word: You are a Cohen (Priest) forever in the same manner as Malki-Tzedek!*

(4) The sacrificial system has changed. Under the original covenant, animal sacrifices were offered. Under the new covenant, Messiah Himself is the sacrifice. This fulfills the foreshadowing of Psalms 40, relating to animal sacrifice because he chose to martyr Himself on our behalf: *6. You have given me understanding that sacrifices* *and grain offerings are not Your desire and sin offerings are not what You have asked of us. 7. So then I said, Behold! I am coming and will bring a scroll of a book that is written about what has happened to me. 8. It is my great joy to do what is pleasant to You my Elohim; and Your Torah-instruction in the very core of my innermost being.*

Chapter 5, Question 1: What, exactly, was accomplished when Yeshua martyred Himself as our Final Sin Sacrifice?

Answer: He overcame "the world" and death.

John 16:33. I have spoken these things to you that in me there may be to you peace. In the world will be affliction to you, but take courage, I have conquered the world.

Chapter 5, Question 2: Colossians 2:14 tells us He (Yeshua) wiped away the "bill of charges" or "our debts" against us. Romans 3:31 says: *Do, we then nullify Torah by faith? May it never be! On the contrary, we establish Torah.* Cite here any scriptures in the Gospels where man was ever told that Torah was abolished.

Answer: There is not one scripture to support the idea that Torah was abolished "at the cross" or anywhere else! Our certificate of debt/bill of charges was "nailed to the cross" – nothing else.

Colossians 2:13. And you who were dead in your sins and by the uncircumcision of your flesh, he has resurrected with him; and he has forgiven us all our sins: 14. and, by his mandates, he blotted out the handwriting of our debts which (handwriting) existed against us, and took (it) from the midst and affixed (it) to his stake. 15. And, by yielding up his body, he showed contempt for principalities and authorities; and put them to shame, openly, in his own person.

Chapter 5, Question 3: Please explain in your own words what the following passage means: Romans 2:13. *For it is not merely the hearers of the Torah whom God considers righteous; rather, it is the doers of what Torah says who will be made righteous in God's sight. 14. For whenever Gentiles, who have no Torah, do naturally what the Torah requires, then these, even though they don't have Torah, for themselves are Torah!*

Answer: Notice how those "under Torah" and those "doers of Torah" are put in opposition to one another; therefore, both cannot simultaneously be in error. This is clarified with the phrase *"for doers of Torah will be made righteous."* So, if Torah-doers are made righteous, it stands to reason Torah itself is not passing away! The fact that such deep pro-Torah statements are being sent to Gentiles in Rome speaks volumes of how mainstream Christianity is perverting Rav Shaul's teachings. "Under Torah" means to look to its rituals as a form of magic; a power that needs no purity of intent to bring about blessing, but merely fixed repetition. Torah in itself provides no authority of magic. Rather, Torah has authority because it is YAHWEH's instruction to man! So "under Torah" is a false teaching that has never been true according to the *Tanakh*: YAHWEH blesses man for Torah observance, which is obedience to His Commandments. Notice in Matthew 15 how Y'shua rebukes the Pharisees on this very issue, how they set aside YAHWEH's Torah (instructions) in favor of their traditions. (Used with permission from the AENT).

Chapter 5, Question 4: Romans 14 says: *5. One man discriminates between days; and another judges all days alike. But let every one be sure in regard to his knowledge. 6. He that esteems a day, esteems (it) for his Master: and he that esteems not a day for his Master, he does not esteem (it). And he that eats, eats to his Master and gives thanks to Elohim: and he that eats not to his Master he eats not and gives thanks to Elohim.* Where or how does this passage suggest that Paul said it is up to each of us to decide what we should eat and what day we should keep?

Answer: The context of this passage was a dispute over whether one can eat food that may or may not have been offered to idols. In those days food that may or may not have been offered to idols was usually put out for sale to people on a certain day of the week – and some believers refused to purchase or eat food on those days, just to be on the safe side. On the other hand, some did because they figured, since they didn't know for sure whether or not it had been offered, it wouldn't be wrong to eat it.

Chapter 5, Question 5: The books of Leviticus and Deuteronomy specify what can and cannot be consumed. Although it may not make sense to most of us, the bottom line is, YAHWEH doesn't want us to consume "garbage disposals" – those animals specifically designed to clean up the bottoms of rivers and oceans and streets and forests by eating other dead animals, etc. Can you name some of those "garbage disposals" and describe why we should adhere to the command today to NOT eat them?

Answer: Swine, shrimp, lobster, crab, crows – anything that eats "anything" including the carcasses of other dead animals. Since they eat things that died of old age, or were killed and might be diseased, eating the animals that ate the diseased "road kill" etc., could make us sick. YAHWEH outlined in Leviticus what constitutes "clean" animals, and it is a sin to go against His commands.

Chapter 5, Question 6: Torah is not for salvation, but for _____.

Answer: Sanctification.

Chapter 5, Question 7: As Acts 28:23 clearly shows, Paul taught from _____.

Answer: Torah!

Chapter 5, Question 8: In your own words, please explain what Peter's vision meant in Acts 11.

Answer: The Torah observant Peter would never have eaten the kosher animals that had been in contact with *treif* (non-kosher) animals. The vision was to show that, as Peter knew which animals were clean and which were not because as God had shown him, Peter was to accept the Gentiles as God had now shown him they were "clean". The rest of the passage in Acts 11 shows that this is the correct interpretation and what the vision was all about (see Acts 11:18).

Chapter 5, Question 9: Where did Rav Sha'ul (Apostle Paul) ever suggest that, since Yeshua's death, we can eat whatever we want, meaning there is no more "Kosher"?

Answer: When read in context, the answer is a resounding "No!" Kosher Law always was, and still is, God's Law. YAHWEH never said pork, shellfish, etc. were food! People called these things food in rebellion against Him. The passages in question within the "New Testament" deal with animals God gave us to eat and whether they are ceremonially clean and can be eaten at that time. Even in Peter's vision (Acts 11), Peter knew which animals he could not eat because he observed Torah. The vision was illustrating that the Gentiles were now to be accepted! The rest of the passage in Acts 11 shows that this is the correct interpretation and what the vision was all about.

Chapter 5, Question 10: How did the death of Yeshua create the idea that "unclean" animals are now considered "clean"?

Answer: It didn't! Yeshua was our Final SIN Sacrifice, not someone who came to change or abolish His Father's Divine rules and regulations.

Chapter 5, Question 11: Was Yeshua Torah observant? Were His disciples and the Apostles? How do you know?

Answer: Absolutely! They kept the Seventh Day Sabbath (Acts 1:12, 13:13, 13:42-44, 15:21-22, 16:13, 17:2, 18:4, etc; Hebrews 4) and the Feasts (Acts 12:4; Luke 22:13; John 18:28; Hebrews 11:28), and worshipped in synagogues (Acts 15:21, 17, 18, 19:8, etc.) – and the only meat we know of that they ate was lamb.

Chapter 5, Question 12: Apostle Paul was caught being Torah observant 29 years AFTER Messiah's death (Acts 21:23-24). And Paul said: *"What will we say then? Is Torah sin? May it never be! For I had not learned sin except by means of Torah: for I had not known lust, had not Torah said, You will not covet"....* (Romans 7:7). He also said: *"Torah is Set Apart; and the Commandment is Set Apart, and righteous, and good."* (Romans 7:12) What then, would make someone believe he spoke against the Torah and suggested Christians don't have to bother with it?

Answer: For some reason, Christians adhere to the misunderstood writings of Paul over and above what Yeshua actually taught. Not once did Paul ever espouse any anti-Torah rhetoric.

Chapter 5, Question 13: If you had to pick one or the other to follow, whose teachings would you pick – Yeshua's or Paul's? Why?

Answer: Yeshua's, of course, because He was the Word of YAHWEH in the flesh!

Chapter 5, Question 14: What is meant by "Unless your righteousness **surpasses** those of the Pharisees and the teachers of the Torah you shall surely not enter into the kingdom of heaven" (Matthew 6:20)? How was righteousness established **at that time** if not by Torah?

Answer: Yeshua would certainly not mention "the Pharisees" in this context, except that they walked in a degree of righteousness. Most ancient and modern Pharisees (Orthodox) have disciplined and righteous lifestyles; therefore Yeshua is stating the difference. As the *Ruach haKodesh* writes Torah upon the hearts of his followers, they will surpass the righteousness of the Pharisees who elevate tradition rather than Torah. Those without Torah have NO righteousness, and they are certainly not "borrowing" any from Mashiyach's righteousness while they continue in sin, regardless of what their theologians have to say. Mashiyach imparts his righteousness to those who follow him, and keep Torah. Through Yeshua, YAHWEH is raising up a Set Apart people who keep His Commandments rather than their own religious traditions.

Question 15: Yeshua said in Matthew 19:17, *"Now if you desire to enter into life, keep the Commandments."* If Christians are "free from the law" as they say, then why does Yeshua *explain* from the commandments of the "Old Testament"? For instance:

*Matthew 5:38. You **have heard that it has been said** that an eye for an eye and a tooth for a tooth. 39. **But I say to you** that you should not stand against evil, but who hits you upon your right cheek, turn also to him the other.*

"You have heard it said" refers to oral tradition and/or man's interpretation of what was written in Torah. But when Yeshua says "I say to you" or "it is written" He is *explaining* the proper meaning of those laws. So, what, exactly, are Christians free from?

Answer: By accepting the God of Abraham, Isaac and Jacob and adhering to HIS commands, we are free from the bondages of sin! Sin no longer has a hold over us because we have chosen to live a holy life by following the commandments of YAHWEH. As humans born into a sinful world, we will always be tempted at some point, but those who know Torah have an "insurance policy" full of holy guidelines that will "prick our consciences" and keep us FROM sinning. Once Torah is written upon our hearts, we are much less likely to commit a willful sin than those who don't know God or His Word very well.

The bottom line is, Torah is freedom! Torah is our blueprint for holy living which shows us how to get a closer relationship with God. If Christians would obey Torah, they would be free from the bondage of sin!

Chapter 5, Question 16: According to the Gospels, the Apostles were not learned scholars. We are told they were fishermen, a tax collector, a tent maker..."blue collar" types. In those days, they had to go through a great ordeal to document their experiences with Yeshua, which included gaining access to Papyrus on which to write down their accounts. As far as we know the only Apostle who could speak a foreign language was Paul, who spoke some Greek. In view of this, do you really believe the Apostles would have written the Gospels in Greek? Why or why not?

Answer: The Gospels were written in Hebrew and Aramaic. There is no evidence that the Apostles wrote the Gospels in anything but the language(s) they spoke. Though the dates of the oldest manuscripts regardless of the language is difficult to determine, the key Greek manuscripts from which most modern translations originate have been assessed from the 350 CE to 500 CE period. The oldest Syriac (Aramaic) manuscripts have been dated to 170 CE – nearly 200 years earlier than the Greek.

Chapter 6, Question 1: Of the "613 Commandments" most cannot be kept today because they were prescribed for the priests and kings of the day, while some were only for men and others for women. However, there were some commandments that were meant to last "forever" and/or they were to be a "permanent ordinance throughout your generations". Can you name some of them?

Answer: The Ten Commandments (Exodus 20); the wearing of *tzitzits* (tassels) (Numbers 15:38); the Seventh Day Sabbath (Genesis 2:2-3, Ezekiel 20:11-12) and the

Biblical Feasts which are spread throughout the year (Leviticus 23).

Chapter 6, Question 2: Since God is the same yesterday, today and forever (Hebrews 13:8), why would He suddenly want us to ignore His feasts/appointed times? Does it make sense that, just because Yeshua died, it would automatically negate the other three feasts He has yet to fulfill? Your thoughts on this?

Answer: Absolutely not! Yeshua was our Final Sin Sacrifice who came to "fulfill" – which meant not to "abolish" but rather to establish/confirm and make happen the prophecies about Himself.

Chapter 6, Question 3: YAHWEH designed His appointed times, the *mo'edim*, for His people to come together to worship Him. The fact that all flesh will one day worship YAHWEH according to one calendar tells us that the *mo'edim* are not for Jews only, but for **all** the Household of Faith as One Body. ("His people" includes anyone who has been "grafted in" to the Olive Tree [Isra'el] to worship the risen Messiah.) Besides the Seventh Day Sabbath which constitutes a "date with God" every Saturday wherein we are to rest from the old week and refresh ourselves for the new, can you name the seven other Feasts which are spread throughout the year and their eternal significance? (Hint: See Leviticus 23.)

Answer:

First and foremost: The Sabbath.

*Ezekiel 20:11. I gave them My statutes and showed them My ordinances, through which if a person obeys them he will have life through them. 12. I gave them My Shabbats to be **a sign between Me and them**, so that they would know that I, YHWH, am the One Who makes them Set-Apart.*

The Feasts:

1. Passover/Pesach (Nisan 14) always falls in the March/April timeframe on the Gregorian calendar: Leviticus 23:5 tells us: *In the first month, on the fourteenth day of that month at twilight, is YHWH's Pesach.*

This Feast celebrates the deliverance of the Hebrew slaves from Egypt. It is a tale of redemption through the killing of the Passover Lamb whose blood was to be applied to the doorposts of their houses – an act which would spare their firstborn from the Tenth Curse against Pharaoh. YAHWEH promised that the Angel of Death would "pass over" those houses with the blood on the doorposts, and spare the first born (Exodus 12:1-13).

This foreshadowed Yeshua, YAHWEH's "Passover Lamb" who fulfilled Passover when he was crucified and willingly allowed His own blood to be shed on our behalf in order to become our redemption. In other words, the innocent died for the guilty; and sacrifice not only means death but also life (Isaiah 53.)

2. Unleavened Bread/Hag HaMatzot (Nisan 15) marks the beginning of a seven day period during which the eating of leavened Bread is forbidden as leaven is a symbol of sin (1 Corinthians 5:6-8, Matthew 16:11-12, Galatians 5:7-9). Messiah Yeshua fulfilled this Feast when he was buried and became our righteousness (Romans 6:4, 2 Corinthians 5:21).

Exodus 23:14-16 says:

Exodus 23:14. Three times a year you are to keep a feast unto Me. 15. You will observe and keep the Feast of Unleavened Bread as I commanded you, at the appointed time when you came out of Egypt in the month of Abib. None of you will appear before Me empty handed. 16. Additionally you will celebrate the feast of the harvest, the first fruits of your work, which you have sowed in the fields. Finally, the Feast of Ingathering at the turn of the year when you gather from the fields your labor.

3. Firstfruits/Yom HaBikkurim (Nisan 16) falls during the March/April timeframe: This Feast, celebrating the bringing of the firstfruits of the winter harvest to the Temple (indicating there will be more to come!) is symbolic of Yeshua being the Firstfruits (1 Corinthians 15:23). His resurrection was a "wave offering" presented to YAHWEH as the firstfruits of the harvest of souls that is yet to come.

4. Feast of Weeks/Shavuot is celebrated during the May/June timeframe. Exodus 34:22 tells us: *And you will keep the Feast of Weeks, that is, the first fruits of the wheat harvest and the Feat of Ingathering at the turn of the year.*

Shavuot falls fifty days after Passover. Torah directs the seven-week Counting of the Omer (which begins on the second day of Passover and culminates after seven weeks, the next day being Shavuot). The counting of the days and weeks conveys anticipation of and desire for the Giving of the Torah. In other words, at Passover, the Israelites were freed from slavery in Egypt; and 50 days later on Shavuot they accepted YAHWEH's Torah which made them a nation committed to serving God.

This Feast was fulfilled by the coming of the promised Ruach HaKodesh (Holy Spirit) on the disciples of Yeshua in the Temple. It represents the beginning of the body of Messiah on Earth in which all believers, redeemed through the blood of Messiah, are lifted up before YAHWEH and set apart as holy (Acts 2, John 14:15-18, Ephesians 2:11-22).

5. Trumpets/Rosh Hashana (Tishri 1) falls in the September/October timeframe: Leviticus 23:23-25 says:

23. And again YHWH spoke to Moshe saying: 24. Speak to the children of Israel saying: In the seventh month on the first day of that month you are to have a Shabbat-style rest consisting of a remembrance through the blowing of trumpets and a Set-Apart reading service. 25. You will not do any menial labor to expand your domain but instead present to YHWH an offering by fire.

It is the Jewish Civil New Year; the anniversary of the creation of Adam and Eve and their first actions toward the realization of man's role in the world; of the first sin that was committed and resulting repentance; a day when YAHWEH takes stock of all of His Creation, which includes all of humanity. During this Feast, the blowing of shofars (rams' horns) signifies the bringing together of God's people, warning them to repent during the coming "days of awe" (the 10 days between Trumpets and the Day of Atonement).

The Feast of Trumpets also signals the call for repentance, for the time is short and Judgment is coming upon the Earth – whether people are ready, or not! (See the Book of Revelation.)

6. Day of Atonement/Yom Kippur (Tishri 10) falls in the September/ October timeframe: Leviticus 16:29-31 tells us:

29. This will be an eternal statute for you: On the tenth day of the seventh month you will humble and afflict your souls and not do any manner of any work at all, whether you are native born or a foreigner who resides with you. 30. For it is on this day that Atonement will be made for you to cleanse you, so that all your sins will be cleansed before YHWH. 31. It is to be a supreme Shabbat of absolute rest for you, that you will humble and afflict your souls. It is a requirement of you for all time.

This Feast represents the need for the sacrifice/sin offering that must be made for the sins of the nation. We're told that Yeshua shall descend to put to an end to the sins of Isra'el who, at that time will call for the Messiah to return and will mourn for the "One who was pierced". This day will be fulfilled upon the Second Coming of Messiah to the Earth (Matthew 23:37-39; Hosea 5:15 thru 6:1-3; Zecheriah 3:8-9, 12:10, 13:1; Ezekiel 16:61-63).

7. Tabernacles/Sukkot (Tishri 15) falls in the September/October timeframe. This Feast is outlined in Deuteronomy 16:13-15, where YAHWEH tells the Israelites:

13. You will celebrate the Feast of Sukkot (Tabernacles) seven days after you have gathered in from your threshing floor and your winepress. 14. And you will rejoice in your Feast--you and your son and daughter and you male and female servants, along with the Levite and the foreigner and the orphan and the widow in your towns. 15. Seven days you will celebrate a feast to YHWH your Elohim in the place that He chooses, for YHWH your Elohim will bless you and all of your produce and in all of the work of your hands, so that your joy will be complete.

Leviticus 23:39-43 says:

39. And precisely on the fifteenth day of the seventh month, when you have brought together all the crops of the land, you will celebrate YHWH's Feast for seven days, resting on both the first and the eighth days. 40. On the first day you will take for yourselves the fruit of the beautiful trees, the branches from the palm trees, the boughs of the thick trees and willows from the brook and then you will rejoice before YHWH for seven days. 41. And you will keep YHWH's feast for those seven days in the year. It is an eternal requirement that you keep it in the seventh month. 42. You will live in sukkah (booths) for seven days--all the native born in Israel must live in booths 43. in order that your future generations may know that I made the children of Israel to live in these booths when I brought them out of the land of Egypt. I am YHWH, your Elohim!

This Feast serves as a reminder of the days in the wilderness when YAHWEH's people were forced to reside in tents/huts or temporary dwellings – a reminder of our temporary lives on Earth. It will be fulfilled by the ingathering of the "Final Harvest" of souls just prior to the setting up of the Kingdom of the Messiah on Earth.

Philippians 2:10-11 tells us in that day Yeshua will reign from Jerusalem and *"every knee should bow, of (beings) in heaven and on earth and under the earth; and that every tongue should confess that Y'shua the Mashiyach is YHWH, to the glory of Elohim his Father."* His Kingdom is to last 1,000 years before the eternal order begins in the "new heaven and new earth" (Revelation 21)!

If you're still unsure that Christians are supposed to observe these feasts, please read Leviticus 25:6-47.

Chapter 6, Question 4: Even if Yeshua did rise on a Sunday, where's the scripture to support that YAHWEH ever said His Sabbath is now supposed to be on the first day (Sunday)?

Answer: There are none! MAN decided to change the Sabbath to Sunday.

Chapter 6, Question 5: In 1 Corinthians 5:7-8, what Feast did Paul tell us to observe?

Answer: Passover - not "Easter" with its paganistic roots. Passover has always been on Nisan 14 since the time Moses helped the Israelites escape from Pharaoh. It doesn't fall on the day Christians celebrate Easter! Yeshua died on Passover and rose exactly three days later on the Sabbath. Easter and Passover have nothing whatsoever in common – not to mention that "Easter" (or "Ishtar") was the name of a pagan deity, so why would YAHWEH honor our celebration of Easter? Has He ever been happy about paganism?

Chapter 6, Question 6: The only Bible version in which you will find the word "Easter" is in Acts 12:4 of the King James Version, which basically renders the entire Book of Acts useless since there was no "Easter" before the death of Yeshua. What, in your own words does "Easter" have to do with His death and resurrection?

Answer: Absolutely nothing.

Ezekiel 8:13. And He said to me, Turn around again and you will see the great abominations that they practice. 14. Then He brought me to the entrance of the northern gate of YHWH's House (Temple) and right there in front me were women weeping for Tammuz! 15. Then He said to me,

*Have you seen this O son of Man (mortal man)? Turn back again and you will behold even greater abominations than these. 16. **Then He brought me to the inner court of YHWH's House—and behold!—at the door of the Temple of YHWH, between the porch and the altar, there were about twenty-five men with their backs to the Temple f YHWH and with their faces turned to the east as they worshipped the sun in the east!** 17. He asked me, have you seen this O son of Man? Is it a casual matter that the house of Yehudah that they practice the abominations that they do here and fill the land with violence and angering me even more? Behold! They are even putting the branch to their nose! 18. Therefore I will act with fury, My eye will spare no one and I will have no compassion. Even if they cry loudly in my ear I will refuse to listen to them.*

Unfortunately, this is the very thing millions of Christians do every Easter Sunday morning! They stand there with rapt faces adoring the sun as it rises in the east, not realizing they are performing the rituals demanded by the mythical and idolatrous goddess Ishtar (Easter). Deceived into believing this is Christian, millions practice the identical form of the ancient sun-worship of the Sun-god BAAL!

The Bible tells us this is the MOST ABOMINABLE of all idolatry in the sight of our Creator! Yet millions of Christians partake in this ritual, never stopping to think about what they're actually doing....

Chapter 6, Question 7: After arriving at this point in your workbook and knowing what you now know, please write down exactly what you think was "abolished" or "negated" after the death of Jesus.

Answer: The need for animal sacrifices to atone for our sins.

Chapter 6, Question 8: Please write down a few thoughts about your particular "denomination" and why you belong to the church you attend.

Answer: This question was designed to get you to contemplate whether you are actually desiring to grow spiritually and do God's will in your life, or whether you just happen to like the ear-tickling sermons espoused by your pastor, or because the church offers numerous social activities, etc.

Chapter 6, Question 9: What denomination did Jesus adhere to?

Answer: None! Yeshua was the Word of YAHWEH made flesh, who came to proclaim the Kingdom of YAHWEH. Yeshua never said "I came to establish a religion!" In fact, Yeshua said *"It is necessary for me to preach to other cities the Kingdom of Elohim, for because this reason I have been sent."* (Luke 4:43.) And *"For I came down from heaven, not to do my will, but to do the will of Him who sent me.* (John 6:38).

Chapter 6, Question 10: What was Jesus' assignment on earth? (What did He come to do?)

Answer: To proclaim the Kingdom of YAHWEH:

Luke 4:43. And Y'shua said to them that, It is necessary for me to preach to other cities the Kingdom of Elohim, for because this reason I have been sent.

Chapter 6, Question 11: Describe in your own words what "works" are, and then outline why you believe that keeping the Seventh Day Sabbath and God's seven Feasts would be considered "works."

Answer: "Works" are our attempts to obtain salvation by following the law without faith. As human beings, we are prone to stumble and fail at some point, which means "works" are fruitless. The sermons presented at the pulpits every Sunday are "works" by the pastor; they have nothing to do with God's instructions to obey the Sabbath or the feasts, or with any kosher eating habits.

YAHWEH never once suggested that we should work our way into heaven. But that has nothing, whatsoever, to do with OBEDIENCE to His Divine Instructions to mankind! He gave us His commands as holy guidelines for the conduct of our lives.

Chapter 6, Question 12: The following email was written by a female Baptist missionary. Can you detect at least five ways her comments are off the mark?

"Jesus is His Name, not "Yeshua" which means, "His Name will not be blotted out or obliterated." And the Word was not printed in Aramaic, it was printed in Greek and for a good reason. Because the True and Living God wanted to make sure that the Pharisees did not change the translation to English and fiddle around with it. Peter, upon this rock I will build my Church, and the gates of hell will not prevail against it!"

Answer:

(1) Our Savior's Name was Yeshua, which in Hebrew means "YAHWEH is Salvation". "Jesus", on the other hand, means nothing. "Jesus" is the English translation of the Latin "Iesus" which itself is translated from the Greek "Iesous". One can only wonder how the original Aramaic spelling of Yeshua became "Iesous" by Greek translators.

(2) "YESHU" (not "Yeshua") was an acronym that stood for (Hebrew: *yimmach shemo vezikhro*), meaning "May his name and memory be blotted out." The Name Yeshua means "YAHWEH is Salvation".

(3) The word was originally written in Hebrew and Aramaic.

(4) The "True and Living God" chose Abraham, Isaac and Jacob – Hebrews - to be the Patriarchs of our faith. Yeshua, who came through the line of David through His mother, Miriam (a Jewess), spoke Hebrew and Aramaic.

(5) What the last sentence refers to is anybody's guess, but Peter was NOT the rock upon which the "church" was built, nor did Yeshua build any church....

Chapter 7, Question 1: After reading the beginning of Chapter 7, do you believe Acts 15 exempts Gentiles from being Torah observant? Why or why not?

Answer: You should conclude there is no exemption for Gentiles from being Torah observant! Same God, same rules. Why would God have different rules for His adopted children? See Numbers 15:13-16.

Chapter 7, Question 2: Should believing Gentiles be circumcised? Why or why not?

Answer: Again, same God, same rules. To explain, Andrew Roth points out in a footnote in the AENT on this very subject: "Torah teaches that we must not rely on our flesh (for dust you are, and to dust shall you return), but that we obey our Father YHWH as His children. We are the real circumcision if we obey YHWH and do His will. [Physical] circumcision counts for nothing if we are unwilling to turn to YHWH's instructions and follow in the steps of His Mashiyach (Jeremiah 9). Rav Shaul repeatedly teaches that circumcision of the heart must come first; circumcision of the flesh can never begin to substitute the perfect work of the Ruach haKodesh."

Chapter 7, Question 3: Do you believe Paul's teachings contradict the teachings of Yeshua – even though Paul was a Torah observant Jew who said that the Law was NOT abolished but, rather, "established"?

Answer: Paul never, ever contradicted Yeshua or Torah! He had no authority to do so. Christianity and Catholicism have taken the writings of Paul and twisted them into something anti-Torah and completely unrecognizable.

Chapter 7, Question 4: Please consult your Bible for this question: What did the woman with the issue of blood in Matthew 9:20-22 touch, and why?

Answer: She touched the edge of His *tallit* where his *tzitzit* were because she trusted that He was the Messiah. Yeshua, like all other Torah observant Jews (including the Apostles!), wore *tzitzit* as a reminder to do the Commandments of YAHWEH, and not seek after what is right in one's own eyes. (See Numbers 15:37-38.) The Hebrew *kanaf* is also found in Malachi 4:2 "...with healing in his *kanaf* (wings)..." See also Zechariah 8:23.

Matthew 9:20. And behold, a woman whose blood was flowing twelve years came from behind him and touched the edge of his clothes. 21. For she was saying to herself "If even I touch only his garment, I will be healed."

Chapter 7, Question 5: After having nearly completed this workbook and knowing what you now know, please write in your own words, why you think Christians are ignoring the Biblical Feasts and the seventh day Sabbath commands (especially since YAHWEH said His Sabbath is a "sign between Him and His people" – Ezekiel 20:12), and why Christians insist YAHWEH changed His mind about "clean" and "unclean" foods.

Answer: This question was designed to make people recognize they have been deceived when it comes to Torah.

Chapter 7, Question 6: Christians are guilty of "adding to" Scripture by coining new terms such as "Trinity" and "Rapture" and celebrating the man-made "holy days" of Christmas and Easter – none of which can be found in the Bible. Can you find any scriptures whatsoever that command us to celebrate the birth or resurrection of the Messiah via the man-made "holy days" of Christmas and Easter? What's more, is it okay to lie to your children about the existence of Santa Claus and egg-laying rabbits? What do these things have to do with Yeshua's birth and death and His purpose for coming?

Answer: For those who want to answer: "It's fun; it's tradition" or even, "my kids know there's no Santa Claus or Easter bunny and our family knows the real reason for the season" then please check the Bible to see what God says about man-made traditions!

You simply won't find Christmas and Easter anywhere in the Bible. Those holidays were man's idea and Satan encouraged us to insert paganistic traditions to lead us away from the Truth. What's more, it is simply not okay to lie to your children about the existence of Santa Claus and egg-laying rabbits. Lying is a sin that breaks the Ninth Commandment. Can you honestly say that you've never said to your kids: "Santa Claus is coming soon to bring you toys, so you'd better be good!" or "Look! The Easter bunny brought you some colored eggs!" Is it okay to tell a "little" lie? Since when? Is human tradition worth the cost of making us guilty of sinning in God's eyes?

Chapter 7, Question 7: According to Joel 2:32 and Acts 2:21, those who are saved will do what?

Answer: They will call on the Name of YAHWEH. Not on Allah or Krishna or the Mahdi, or even "Jesus" because that's NOT His Name!

Chapter 8, Question 1: After having finished all eight chapters of this workbook, do you still feel that "the law is a curse? Why or why not?

Answer: Hopefully by now you can conclude: No. His Torah was NEVER a curse! It is a blessing because, without it, we would have no blueprint for moral, holy living. YAHWEH wasn't "cursing" man when He told Moses to present the Divine commandments for His people to live by! The commandments contained within Torah taught man right from wrong and showed us how to obey God and worship Him properly.

Chapter 8, Question 2: What, exactly, is the "curse of the Law"?

Answer: "The curse" is our endeavor to acquire salvation by following the law without faith because, as mere human beings with limited human mindsets, we are prone to stumble at some point:

James 2:8. And if in this you fulfill the Torah of Elohim, as it is written, You will love your neighbor as yourself, you will do well: 9. but if you have partiality towards persons, you commit sin; and you are convicted by Torah as breakers of Torah. 10. For he that will keep the whole Torah and yet fail in one aspect of it, is an enemy to the whole Torah. 11. For he who said, "You will not commit adultery," said also, "You will not kill." If then you commit no adultery, but you do murder, you have become a defiler of Torah. 12. So speak and so act as persons that are to be judged by the Torah of perfect freedom. 13. For judgment without mercy will be on him who has practiced no mercy: by mercy, you will be raised above judgment.

Chapter 8, Question 3: Matthew 5:19 says: *"All who loosen, therefore, from one (of) these small commandments and teach thus to the sons of man, will be called little in the Kingdom of Heaven, but all who do and teach this will be called great in the Kingdom of Heaven."* This passage seems to indicate a hierarchy in heaven showing that those who teach against Torah will be relegated to a much lesser status. How, then, can Christianity justify that Torah has been abolished?

Answer: It seems the context of this passage has been overlooked, misunderstood, or ignored.

Chapter 8, Question 4: Matthew 7:21-23 discusses how YAHWEH will reject the "workers of lawlessness." Who are the "workers of lawlessness"?

Answer: Those who are without "the law." This includes Christianity and Catholicism and all those who refuse to acknowledge Torah.

Chapter 8, Question 5: Please read Matthew 22:37-40. Do these verses in any way suggest the other many commands are now null and void?

Answer: Matthew 22:37-40, read in context, means that if we love God with all our hearts, we will do whatever it takes to follow His Torah.

The Torah and Prophets hang or "hold on by" these two great commandments of Love. Those who do the Commandments, are they who love YAHWEH (Matt 19:17; 1 John 5:2-3). Without love, observance of Torah is vanity, and without Torah, one's "love" is vanity.

Without YAHWEH's divine instructions, Man is totally lost! There were and are and always will be parts of Torah which God said would endure FOREVER....

2 Timothy 3:16. **All Scripture** *that was written by the Spirit is profitable for instruction and for decisive refutation, and for correction, and for deep extensive learning in righteousness; 17.* **that the man of Elohim may become perfect and complete** *for every good work.*

This verse from the *Brit Chadasha* (New Testament) says "ALL scripture is God-breathed"; it doesn't say, "All scripture except for the Torah...."

Chapter 8, Question 6: Many Christians insist they don't have to bother with those "Old Testament commands" because "Jesus has written the law on our hearts." *Without referring to the Bible*, can you name at least five of the Ten Commandments?

Answer. You should be able to list at least five of the following:

1. **Belief in God:** *Exodus 20:2. I am YHWH your Elohim Who brought you out of the land of Egypt and away from the house of slavery.*

2. **Prohibition of Improper Worship:** *Exodus 20:3. You will have no other elohim besides Me. 4. You will not make for yourself an idol in the for anything that exists in the heavens above or on the earth beneath or in the waters below. 5. You will not bow down to them or worship them because I, YHWH, your Elohim, am a jealous Elohim, punishing the children for the sins of their fathers to the third and fours generation of those who hate me 6. but showing love to a thousand generations of those who love Me and keep My commandments.*

3. **Prohibition of Oaths:** *Exodus 20:7. You will not bring the Name of YHWH your Elohim to desolation through substitution (with other gods), because YHWH will punish anyone who abuses His Name.*

4. **Shabbat:** (This encompasses all commandments related to the Sabbath, holidays, or sacred time.) *Exodus 20:8. Remember the Shabbat day to keep it Set-Apart (from the rest of the week). 9. Six days will you work to expand your domain, 10. but the seventh day is the Shabbat unto YHWH your Elohim. You must not do any of your normal work to expand your domain--not you, nor your son, nor your daughter, not your male or female servant, nor your livestock nor any foreigner residing with you within your gates. 11. Because in six days YHWH your Elohim made the heavens and the earth and the seas and all who live there and then He stopped work on the seventh day. Therefore YHWH has blessed the Shabbat and set it apart (from the rest of the week).*

5. **Respect for Parents:** *Exodus 20:12. Give all honor to your father and your mother, that your time in the land YHWH your Elohim is giving you will be of long duration.*

6. **Prohibition of Murder:** *Exodus 20:13. You will not commit murder.*

7. **Prohibition of Adultery:** *Exodus 20:14. You will not commit adultery.*

8. **Prohibition of Theft:** *Exodus 20:15. You will not steal.* (Includes outright robbery as well as other forms of theft, deception, unethical business practices, kidnapping, etc.)

9. **Prohibition of False Witness:** *Exodus 20:16. You will not give false testimony against your fellow citizens.*

10. **Prohibition of Coveting:** *Exodus 20:17. You will not covet your neighbor's house or his wife or his male and female servants, or his ox or his donkey or in fact anything that belongs to your neighbor.*

Chapter 8, Question 7:   Second Timothy 3:16-17 says: *All Scripture that was written by the Spirit is profitable for instruction and for decisive refutation, and for correction, and for deep extensive learning in righteousness; that the man of Elohim may become perfect and complete for every good work.*   Do you believe "all scripture" includes the "Old Testament" scriptures as well? Why or why not?

Answer: Absolutely! The *Tanakh* contains ALL of YAHWEH's "God-breathed", "thus saith the Lord" scriptures. Yeshua quoted and taught from the Tanakh! Without the teaching and instruction of the "Old Testament" what would Yeshua have taught?

Chapter 8, Question 8:   Please read Romans 11:11 and write down exactly **who** will end up causing the Jews to become "jealous" and why.

Romans 11:11. But I say: Have they so stumbled as to fall entirely? May it never be! Rather, by their stumbling, life has come to the Gentiles for (awakening) their jealousy.

Answer: Please note it is the **Gentiles** who will awaken the jealousy of the Jews, not the "Christians." The Gentiles spoken of here are those who have accepted YAHWEH and His Torah and are being obedient.   Traditional Jews will **never** be jealous of a Torah-less, Christmas and Easter celebrating, pork and shellfish eating Christian, because believing Jews fear Elohim enough to know that they will NEVER forsake His Torah.

While this might sound a bit blunt, it only makes sense that those who are Torah observant believers in YAHWEH and His Son Yeshua KNOW, beyond that proverbial shadow of a doubt, that it would be a death knell to heed any type of paganistic theology. YAHWEH warned His People, time and time again:

Deuteronomy 7: (Moses, speaking to the Hebrews) 6. For you are a people Set-Apart for YHWH your Elohim. YHWH your Elohim has selected you from all the peoples of the earth to be His own precious treasured possession. 7. It was not you were the most numerous of all the nations that YHWH set His heart towards you and chose you. Quite the opposite—since you were the smallest of all the peoples! 8. Rather, because YHWH loved you and kept account of His oath which He swore to your ancestors, YHWH then brought you out with a strong hand and redeemed you from the house of bondage from under the hand of Pharaoh, ruler of Egypt.

1 Corinthians 12:1. And concerning spiritual matters, my Brothers, I would have you know, 2. That you have been pagans; and have been, without distinction, led away after idols in which there is no speech.

Matthew 6:6. But when you pray enter your inner room and close your door and pray to your Father who is in secret and your Father who sees in secret He will reward you in open. 7. And when you pray, you should not be chatterers like the pagans, for they hope that by many words they will be heard. 8. Therefore, do not imitate them for your Father knows what need you have before you ask Him.

NOTE: Prayer is a *dialogue* with Heaven, not a monologue. Yeshua's teaching stands as the demarcation between relationship with YAHWEH rather than a religion about Him. Prayer is meant to establish and maintain an intimate relationship, and accountability between each individual and YAHWEH.

Chapter 8, Question 9: In view of the above, do you think it's a good idea to tell a Jewish person they will go to hell if they don't believe in Jesus? Why or why not?

Answer: No. First of all, nobody has the authority to decide whether or not anyone will go to hell because YAHWEH knows our hearts and only He knows who has accepted Him. Secondly, "Jesus" is a Torah-less Christian entity who in no way resembles the actual Messiah who walked the earth 2,000 years ago, and to attempt to force Jews to believe in Jesus is, in effect, leading them AWAY from the Truth of YAHWEH and His Torah.

Chapter 8, Question 10: The prophet Micah asked: "With what shall I come before YAHWEH and bow down to Elohim from on high?" (Micah 6:6) What should your answer be?

Answer: If you're one of the few who has actually grasped the concept of Torah in your journey through this book, then the answer to Micah's question should have been crystal clear: "My total obedience to Him and His Torah! No more excuses, no more willingness to follow man's ideology or theology, and no more paganism!"

Psalms 119:33 Teach me, O YHWH, the path of Your statutes and I will guard it for its own sake. 34 Give me discernment and I will watch over and keep Your Torah-instruction and preserve it with all of my heart.

As sad as it might sound, because of their refusal to accept Torah, the typical Christian pastor has renounced being holy and "Set Apart" unto YAHWEH, as this requires following in the footsteps of Mashiyach who led by example to show us how to do it.

Chapter 8, Question 11: At this point in your studies you should recognize the fact that the original followers of Yeshua and His disciples were all Torah observant and that Christianity was borne out of Catholicism which had totally twisted the teachings of Yeshua. That being the case, how can today's Christians claim that their respective churches are the "original church that Jesus built" when none of them observe Torah, and most of them ignore the seventh day Sabbath and the Biblical feasts? Does your church in any way resemble anything that Yeshua originally taught? Please check the Bible thoroughly before answering.

Answer: Throughout the *Tanakh*, Gentiles were considered to be immoral heathens and pagans because they worshipped every kind of "god" except for YAHWEH. But yet, it was YAHWEH's will for the Gentile nations to receive His Salvation (Isaiah 49:6, 42:6). He told Abraham that through him all the nations of the earth would be blessed (Genesis 12:1-3). Early believing Jews didn't understand this, and at first proclaimed the Good News of the Messiah only to Jewish people. Consequently, the controversy in the First Century was not **if** it was Jewish to believe in Yeshua but whether Gentiles could be included without having to become Jewish (addressed by the Jerusalem council – Acts 15:1-31).

Chapter 8, Question 12: If you are among the few fully grasping the concept of Torah and, **if** as a result, you decide to become Torah observant, be prepared for some major persecution from those who cannot or will not see. Many, if not most, Christians will fight you to the death over the idea of "the law". Once the persecution comes, all you can do is to cling to the Word and ask yourself: "Whom will I follow – God or man and mammon?" After reading this workbook, what will your answer be?

Answer: No question about it, if we belong to YAHWEH, we must follow Him!

Some final thoughts to ponder:

Yeshua is our "New Covenant" and "Final Sin Sacrifice" who was the Word of YAHWEH in the flesh. YAHWEH gave us a New **Covenant**, not a new Torah! As you have now discovered, He did not make a "new covenant" with the Gentiles, but with Houses of Judah and Isra'el who were and still are Torah observant because that is what YAHWEH commanded of His People.

Yeshua's blood sacrifice covers only your past sins and the ones you unintentionally/inadvertently commit today - sins that are committed in ignorance (Hebrews 9:7). Sins against Torah (which you are supposed to know and **obey** since it is "written on our hearts" – Jeremiah 31:32, Deuteronomy 11:18, 2 Corinthians 3:2-3) are **not** covered! This is why Paul spent so much time in Hebrews explaining the meaning of Yeshua's death. Yeshua did not die so that, once we have accepted Him as our Savior, we could continue to sin on purpose.

"Mercy" and "Grace" do NOT invalidate Torah!

* * * * * * *

Thank you so much for participating in this study. My prayer is that you have grasped the concept about Torah and are now ready and willing to apply it to your own lives. Once you get started, you will "feel" more blessed and closer to God than ever before!

May He richly bless you as you continue to learn about and grow in Him!

www.ingramcontent.com/pod-product-compliance
Lightning Source LLC
Chambersburg PA
CBHW062059090426

42741CB00015B/3278